PSYCHOLOGY LIBRARY EDITIONS:
SOCIAL PSYCHOLOGY

Volume 16

PSYCHO-ANALYSIS AND SOCIAL PSYCHOLOGY

PSYCHO-ANALYSIS AND SOCIAL PSYCHOLOGY

WILLIAM MCDOUGALL

Psychology Press
Taylor & Francis Group
LONDON AND NEW YORK

First published in 1936

This edition first published in 2015
by Psychology Press
27 Church Road, Hove BN3 2FA

and by Psychology Press
711 Third Avenue, New York, NY 10017

Psychology Press is an imprint of the Taylor & Francis Group, an informa business

British Library Cataloguing in Publication Data
A catalogue record for this book is available from the British Library

ISBN: 978-1-138-83092-9 (Set)
ISBN: 978-1-315-69455-9 (Set) (ebk)
ISBN: 978-1-138-85253-2 (Volume 16) (hbk)
ISBN: 978-1-315-72342-6 (Volume 16) (ebk)

Publisher's Note
The publisher has gone to great lengths to ensure the quality of this reprint but points out that some imperfections in the original copies may be apparent.

Disclaimer
The publisher has made every effort to trace copyright holders and would welcome correspondence from those they have been unable to trace.

PSYCHO-ANALYSIS AND SOCIAL PSYCHOLOGY

by

WILLIAM McDOUGALL, M.B., F.R.S.

PROFESSOR OF PSYCHOLOGY IN DUKE UNIVERSITY; FORMERLY PRESIDENT OF THE SOCIETY FOR PSYCHICAL RESEARCH AND OF THE PSYCHIATRIC SECTION OF THE ROYAL SOCIETY OF MEDICINE

METHUEN & CO. LTD. LONDON

36 *Essex Street W.C.*

First published in 1936

PRINTED IN GREAT BRITAIN

PREFACE

In these few lectures delivered in the University of London (May 1935) I have returned to the always interesting, but generally quite futile, task of criticizing the teachings of Professor Sigmund Freud and his school. On the present occasion my criticisms are made with ruthless frankness, in accordance with the policy I have recently adopted. I have realized too late that I might have done much more for my chosen science, had I from the first spoken with a less modest voice. It seems to me probable that, had I at the outset put forward my views in a more self-assertive and clamant fashion, I might have been acknowledged as the leader of a powerful and perhaps dominant school of psychology; instead of remaining a well-nigh solitary outsider playing a lone hand; I might even have 'put over' the type of psychology which I believe to be most nearly true, and to be indispensable for the advance of all the social sciences.[1] For, in psychology, far more than in any other field of science, the prestige and authority of a like-minded group would seem to be essential to the success of any theory or system.

[1] In this connexion I must gratefully mention one exception, at least: namely, my near and dear colleague, Dr. Helge Lundholm.

But if my criticism is ruthless, it is nevertheless entirely friendly; and it aspires to be constructive. If from among all the rival systems of psychology I have singled out as the object of my critical attack the system of Freud, it is not that I regard his views as more in need of criticism than any other, it is rather because I hold Freud's system to be the most deserving of honest criticism, to have the essential foundations of truth that are lacking in most other contemporary systems, to be, in short, nearer than any other to the system elaborated by myself; and also because Freud himself, with true greatness, has shown in his later works, and especially in his last book, that he also can see defects in his system and can make important changes and improvements in it.

Frankly, then, these lectures are published in the hope of hastening the fusion of these two closely allied and complementary systems, a fusion or synthesis which, while rejecting the errors of both systems, shall combine the best features of both.

The most essential features of my own system were sketched in my *Introduction to Social Psychology* (written in 1907, before I had made acquaintance with Professor Freud's writings, and first published in 1908). Although that little book has reached its twenty-second edition, very few of my colleagues have recognized that it contains something more than a list of instincts, contains in fact, under the guise of a theory of the sentiments, the first systematic sketch of the structure of character and a theory of its development from native tendencies under the moulding pressure of social traditions. It is especially to this most fundamental and original part of my system that Freud's later studies have led him to approach more and more nearly, and it has been his ventures into the province of Social Psychology which have led him in this direction.

Shortly after the delivery of these lectures, Professor C. E. M. Joad published an article in *The New Statesman* entitled ' Psychology in Retreat '. In that article (which provoked a multitude of replies and protests) he misrepresented me as sharing with him a belief traditional with the philosophers of Oxford, namely, that the methods of science are not applicable to the study of mind and that scientific psychology is therefore an impossibility. This is not the first occasion on which Mr. Joad, to serve his journalistic needs, has grossly misrepresented me ; and I beg to protest. If I spoke gloomily of the present state of psychology, it was because we, the psychologists of the present generation, have so lamentably failed to reach agreement on the fundamentals of our science ; a failure which in my lectures I attributed emphatically to the poverty of our intellectual powers and not to any radical and intrinsic inapplicability of scientific method to human problems.

In another small volume, *World Chaos*, I have insisted on the world's urgent need for more and better psychologists who shall provide the indispensable foundation for all the Social Sciences and, in so doing, shall make themselves the saviours of our collapsing civilization. I stand by that proclamation and yield to no man in my estimation of the benefits that may accrue to mankind if only sufficiently high intellectual powers can be concentrated co-operatively in the scientific attack on the problems of human nature. I would go so far as to say that, at the present juncture of human affairs, two studies only are of real importance, namely: Religion and Psychology. For it is these two closely allied studies that must teach us the answers to the old questions—What am I? What may I hope for? What ought I to do?

The first four Appendices are reprints of articles previously published in *Mind*, in the *Journal of Abnormal and Social Psychology*, and in *Archives of Neurology and Psychiatry*. To the editors of these journals I return thanks for their kind permission to re-publish.

W. McD.

December 1935

CONTENTS

APPENDICES

CHAPTER I

AN ESTIMATE OF PROGRESS AND PROSPECTS[1]

CHOICE OF TOPIC AND GROUNDS THEREOF

It is obvious that in these three lectures I can deal with only a small part of the now vast field of psychological inquiry. I must choose some one of its many subdivisions. And I choose Social Psychology and its relations with psycho-analytic doctrines. My choice is determined by two considerations: first, the psycho-analytic movement initiated and inspired by Freud has done more than any other to interest the intelligent public in psychology, it is held in higher esteem by that public than any other psychological teaching, and, in spite of its many errors (as I think), it has made very real contributions.

Secondly, social psychology is the most concrete branch of the science of human nature and therefore the most significant for such a review as I here attempt. It alone does not abstract from the social setting, the multitude of social influences which surround and constantly play upon

[1] The substance of three Lectures delivered to the London University in June 1935.

every human being from womb to tomb. By reason of this highly concrete nature, Social Psychology is the best testing-field for psychological theories ; its problems serve as touchstones for theories. No doubt the ultimate test of our theories must be the application of them as guides to practical endeavour in such fields as medicine and education. But in these fields, and especially in psychological medicine, the relations between causes and effects are very complex, very difficult to trace ; consequently, the processes of pragmatic verification are very liable to error.

Hence, in the present early stage of the development of psychology, the extension of theories to the problems of social life affords a better test of their validity than does their practical application in medicine, education, industry, or other field of practical social effort. The principle may be illustrated by reference to the problem of *suggestion.* Suggestion is a process which can be wholly ignored by psychologists so long as they are not concerned with social life ; and, as a matter of history, for a very long time it was so ignored ; and especially the very striking and immensely instructive phenomena of suggestion working on the hypnotic subject were thrust on one side as curiosities, monstrosities, or fraudulent displays ; and even to this day there are many professors of psychology who ignore them, shun them, or even deny them. But, as soon as psychology began to concern itself with social phenomena, it became obvious that suggestion pervades social life in its every part and aspect; and it became hardly less obvious that any theory of human nature (such as pure associationism or 'stimulus-response behaviourism') which stands helpless before the problem of suggestion, is at once revealed as utterly untenable.

THE NEED OF SOME TOUCHSTONE FOR THEORIES

Recognition of this principle, the principle of testing out psychological systems by their adequacy in the field of social phenomena, is much needed; especially the rising generation of psychologists need to use this principle as their guide in choosing, among the many rival systems, the form of psychology most deserving to be adopted and actively supported.

When I look back upon my own career in psychology, the need of conscious adoption of some such principle is brought home to me vividly. Since early youth I have devoted my energies intensively to the effort to learn something about human nature. For many years I felt I was wandering in the wilderness without landmarks, without sure guides, without any sure principles for finding my way. Even now after some forty-five years of sustained effort, I am not sure that I have made any progress, have learnt anything of human nature. As truly as any man now living, I may say with the poet:

Myself when young did eagerly frequent
Doctor and Saint, and heard great argument
About it and about: but evermore
Came out by the same door where in I went.

With them the Seed of Wisdom did I sow
And with mine own hand wrought to make it grow;
And this was all the harvest that I reap'd—
'I came like Water, and like Wind I go'.

It is true that a certain scheme of human nature now seems to me preferable to all others: but, among all the multitude of my fellow-students, perhaps five in a hundred would give a much qualified approval of that scheme, while the other ninety-five per cent would regard me as utterly and wholly in error.

I can see several lines of contemporary research which seem to me fruitful; but, again, a vast majority of our colleagues regard each of these with incredulous contempt. Can I, then, confidently set up my own judgement in flat opposition to the overwhelming majority of my fellow-students? I ask myself—Who am I that I should thus presume to be in the right? I find myself driven to ask very seriously—Are we making any progress towards that systematically organized knowledge of human nature which psychology aspires to be? And sometimes, pondering this question, I incline to accept the answer long current among the philosophers of Oxford, in the midst of whom for fifteen years I lived and moved and had my being; the answer namely: No, it is not possible to attain to such knowledge ; the science implied by the word ‘ psychology ’ is beyond our reach ; no such science exists and no such science is possible to us.

But I feel sure that, if this answer is the true one, if scientific knowledge of human nature is not to be attained, that is not due to any intrinsic impossibility, any radical inadequacy of the scientific method ; but is rather due to the lack in us of sufficiently developed intellectual powers.[1] And the more fully acquainted I become with the history of psychology, the more I am inclined to this pessimistic conclusion, namely, the mental powers of our species are inadequate to the task of building up the science of human nature.[2]

THE DEPLORABLE CONDITION OF PSYCHOLOGY

The present condition of psychology is deplorable. And, in important respects, the condition is more deplorable now than it was fifty or one hundred years ago, or indeed at any earlier period you may name. For, if we look at the state of psychology one hundred years ago, one may say that the scientific method was still in its infancy,

[1] I here emphasize this sentence, because Professor Joad, misinterpreting my remarks, initiated a lively discussion in the press by writing an article entitled ‘ Psychology in Retreat ’, in which he defended the traditional view of the Oxford philosophers.

[2] For the last fifteen years I have studied that history intensively, and am in fact engaged in writing a history of psychology.

was only in process of being achieved. And fifty years ago, although the scientific method was pretty well developed and understood and had achieved immense successes in other fields, no sustained and concerted endeavour to apply it to the problems of human nature had been made. Whereas at the present time we can make no such excuse, no such justification of our continuing ignorance, no such explanation of our lack of any generally accepted body of established knowledge. For the last twenty years at least, the workers have been very numerous and active, and the mass of publication enormous : yet the chaos continues and grows worse ; serious divergences of principle are more numerous and more acute ; the hope of agreement seems to grow fainter.

Nor does Psychology seem to be appreciably nearer to recognition as a science of any importance, whether by the scientific world in general, by the workers in the various social sciences (which so urgently need an assured and agreed psychological foundation), or by the educated general public. We occasionally find an enthusiast acclaiming the progress of Psychology ; as when Professor Seligman, in his recent Huxley Lecture,[1] speaks of ' the vast advances in psychology of recent years '. But if challenged to point to any advances (other than of bare facts) regarded

[1] ' Anthropological Perspective and Psychological Theory ', *Journal of Royal Anthropological Institute*, vol. lxii. December, 1933.

as such by a bare majority of psychologists, he would I think be wholly at a loss.[1]

Let me remind you that a century ago James Mill expressed the view that psychology, even then, was a science so far advanced as to be well-nigh perfected and complete. And since his time many others have entertained similar delusions about the progress and high state of development of psychology.

On the other hand, I will point to a recent popular survey of modern science by a very competent hand, that of Mr. J. W. N. Sullivan.[2] He devotes a chapter to our knowledge of the mind ;

[1] It is clear that Professor Seligman, when he speaks of the vast advance of psychology, has in mind the psychology of Professor Freud. Yet when he comes to psychological interpretation of primitive behaviour the principle he chiefly and almost exclusively uses is ' dissociation ', one which is not recognized or used by Freud and his disciples. This incident illustrates a feature of the present situation which is the ground of this illusion of progress, namely : many active minds have thrown out a multitude of suggestions, hypotheses, speculations. Any worker in one or other of the human sciences who has some desultory acquaintance with recent psychological writings, can, like Professor Seligman, with the aid of a little ingenuity, pick up out of the hodge-podge an assortment which will lend themselves to the interpretation of the particular assortment of phenomena in which he is interested; and this may seem more or less satisfactory so long as no demand is made for systematic coherence, order and consistency.

[2] *The Limitations of Science.* London, 1934. In this passage, as in all other citations of this volume, italics are mine, where no contrary indication appears.

and that chapter consists of a demonstration of the absurdities of Watsonian behaviourism, some reference to the obscurities and confusions of the psycho-analytic schools, and a brief mention of the inadequacy of the *Gestalt* doctrines as a system of psychology. There is no mention whatsoever of psychology of any other type. And he sums up by saying—

> '*Certainly there is no generally accepted body of psychological doctrine.* There are, rather, a number of different theories, each having a limited range of application and, where they profess to deal with the same phenomena, differing profoundly from one another.'

After long watching the reactions of the educated public towards psychology, I can testify that Mr. Sullivan's sketch accurately represents its opinion.

I will cite one other similar piece of evidence; namely, a recent book consisting of twenty-two essays written by twenty-two more or less eminent authors, and all directed to the task of answering the question—What is Patriotism? Now that is purely and wholly a psychological question; and, if psychology and psychologists were regarded by the public as having anything of value to teach or to reveal, at least half of the contributors to such a symposium would surely be professed psychologists of one sort or another; especially may we assume this in view of the fact that psychologists are now almost as common as blackberries, and the editor or publisher who merely shot into the brown could hardly fail to hit a few of them. Yet not one of the authors has the slightest claim to be regarded as a psychologist. A book like this means more than a sheer indifference to psychology: it means that editor, publisher and twenty-two authors have a positive contempt for psychology.

No! Professor Seligman is repeating the error of James Mill. The public would be quite at a loss to understand what he means by 'the vast advances of psychology in recent years'; and he would be quite unable to substantiate his claim. If he doubts it, let him try. For the public demands, and rightly, that, before a science can claim to have made any advance in any particular respect, the alleged advance must be recognized and accepted by a majority, or at least by a substantial minority, of the professional workers in that science. And that is just what we cannot claim for any of the alleged advances of recent psychology.

I do not think that I am expressing a merely temperamental or a jaundiced view, nor a discouragement arising from personal lack of success. I am naturally of hopeful temper, my digestion is pretty good, and I have enjoyed a reasonable degree of professional success. It is rather that, after long consideration, I am convinced of the need for a ruthless facing of the situation and an utter frankness in stating the case as I see it. I have until recently been diplomatic and willing to connive at concealing our skeletons. But I have become at last convinced that the position is desperate and that our only hope lies in frankly exposing the facts to ourselves and to the world in general. At the risk of making myself very unpopular, I adopt the policy of ruthless out-speaking.

THE NECESSITY OF THEORY

Let us return now to our young psychologist who aspires to add to our knowledge of human nature by a life of teaching and research in psychology. He finds himself in the midst of a chaos of conflicting theories, or types of theories, of human nature, each claiming his adhesion as the sole road to understanding and progress. His first decision should be whether or no he shall attempt to choose between these rival claimants. Now in the great majority of cases (in America at least where students of psychology are most numerous and where the facts are best known to me) this decision is never made; rather, the actual course of the student is determined by default of decision; he drifts along, never facing up to the problem; he gets busy on some specialized bit of research which brings him his Ph.D. degree; he becomes one of the 1,500 members of the American Psychological Association or of the 1,000 members of the British Psychological Society; perhaps he becomes a professor and drifts on for the rest of his life, never knowing where he stands or what he believes. And in this course of drifting, he is encouraged and abetted by the eminent leaders of psychology in that university which is not only the largest in the world, but also exerts in our field and especially in the field of educational psychology a vastly predominant and, as I think, a deplorable influence in almost all parts of the world. I mean, of course, Columbia University in New York City. There Professors Woodworth and Murphy and Thorndike, whose text-books are vastly more read throughout the world than any others, encourage the drifting process. They say in effect—' Don't worry about theories ; just go on piling up facts. All theories are equally useless and about equally true or untrue. For all practical purposes you may assume that man is merely a machine ; but it is better not to say so outright.'

THE POLICY OF DRIFT

Now I am convinced that this policy of drift is disastrous. I hold that the wide prevalence of this attitude of pusillanimous and contemptuous neutrality towards all theories is largely responsible for the disappointing state of psychology at the present time. It is intellectually and morally deplorable. It robs psychology of all its value as an intellectual discipline ; and it leads nowhere. It is sterilizing for research and paralysing for the teacher. It encourages intellectual shiftlessness and flabbiness, a spineless contentment in a wilderness full of mysteries presented to eyes that are blind to their challenge. Better, and I say it emphatically, better the crudest of theories than no theory at all ; better by far be a J. B. Watson than a Woodworth ; better a blinkered Freudian, led by the nose and repeating mechanically the master's incantations and formulae, than one of the many who combine in their accounts of human nature snippets of Freud, of Jung and of Adler, of Köhler and Koffka and Lewin, of Titchener and of Spearman, with bald behaviourism and the dogma of the S–R bonds. For one can respect the persons and the work of any of the teachers indicated ; but, as my dear friend, Morton Prince, used to say, the man who pretends to accept and combine the doctrines of both Freud and Watson is a fool, and a poor fool at that. His mind is merely a muddle. He forgoes the one great advantage which the study of psychology, with all its drawbacks, can and should bring to its devotees : namely, the stimulus, the privilege and the discipline of wrestling perpetually with great problems, problems that have vexed the minds of great men all down the ages since men began to think.

SOCIAL PROBLEMS AS TOUCHSTONE FOR THEORIES

Suppose now our young psychologist, having decided that he must make a choice, follows the prescription I recommend ; he weighs the merits of the different psychologies, of the various systems and theories, by noting their degrees of success in dealing with the problems of social psychology. What does he find? First and foremost, he will observe that the social sciences, after two generations of disappointed expectations, expectations raised by the introduction of laboratory methods sixty years ago, are turning away from the much-heralded modern scientific psychologies of our academies to create for themselves, as best they may, the foundations of psychological theory that are indispensable to them; and are achieving such mild and harmless products as Professor Spranger's *Lebensformen*,[1] or such a pretentious and muddled system of pseudo-psychology as is contained in Vilfredo Pareto's enormous book, *Traité Générale de Sociologie*.

Next he may note, as I noted with dismay thirty-five years ago, that Wundt's monumental *Völker-Psychologie* was written not at all in terms of his painfully elaborated systematic psychology, but merely in terms of the psychology of common sense and common speech. Similarly, if he goes on to inquire—How does mechanical 'behaviourism' deal with social problems? he may find the answer succinctly given in a text-book of Social Psychology which is representative of many others, that by F. A. Allport. He will

[1] In Berlin, I am told by a recent observer, the general public understands by psychology, not the doctrines of Freud, nor yet those of its own school of *Gestalt*, but Spranger and his *Lebensformen*.

find several chapters which present succinctly the dogmas of strict behaviourism ; while the later and larger part of the book discusses a variety of social problems in the purposive language of common sense and usage, without the least attempt to apply the mechanical principles of the introductory chapters. The fact that this book is used much more widely than any other is one of the signs of the times. It is only one of the many similar books which show a flagrant indifference to all consistency of principle and whose wide circulation implies a similar demoralizing indifference on the part of a multitude of workers, both teachers and students, in our field. But especially our young psychologist may draw the valid conclusion that mechanical behaviourism is quite helpless in face of the problems of social psychology. And his conclusion will be confirmed, if he should apply the special test case, the touchstone, of the phenomena of suggestion.

He may go on to notice that the late Professor Titchener strongly deprecated all attempts to apply psychology to social and practical problems ; for his own peculiar system was utterly and manifestly incapable of interpreting the facts of social life.

He may also observe that a very recent article by Dr. Kurt Lewin [1] represents the first attempt of the *Gestalt* school to enter the field of Social Psychology. And whatever opinion he may form

[1] *Character and Personality*, April 1935.

of the success of this particular attempt to apply the ambiguous quasi-mechanical ways of thinking of the *Gestalt* school, he may observe that the article contains very little *Gestalt* and much *Topologie*, a method that has no essential relation to the *Gestalt* principles.

Let him then turn to the psycho-analytic schools and he will find that the psycho-analysts manifest no reluctance to enter the field of Social Psychology, to submit their doctrines to the testing ground of social problems; that in fact they luxuriate in that field and claim in it many of their most striking successes. Unlike so many of the other psychologies that enjoy, or have recently enjoyed, some vogue, all the psychologies that derive from Freud have proved immediately applicable to a great variety of social problems, and that without undergoing any miraculous transformation of principles or of terminology. Even the much-despised *Individual Psychology* of Dr. Alfred Adler shares this virtue; and by reason of it, is able, in spite of its lack of any vestige of scientific quality, in spite of total disregard for logic, truth, consistency, and coherence, to establish itself as a popular cult, with various centres in Europe and America. It has probably a larger following among the general public than all forms of academic psychology together. It is highly significant that these theories of human nature, devised *de novo* and independently for the interpretation of facts of individual pathology, prove themselves capable of being extended to the interpretation in considerable detail of a wealth of social problems ; and with strikingly close adherence to their own peculiar terminology and ways of thinking.

THE FIELD OF SOCIAL PROBLEMS A MEETING GROUND FOR PSYCHO-ANALYSIS AND SOCIAL PSYCHOLOGY

We must recognize in these facts evidence of some fundamental virtue common to all of these allied doctrines. And social psychologists who, like Professor Knight Dunlap in his recent volume, *Civilized Life*,[1] brush them all aside with a few contemptuous words, are following a short-sighted policy. Rather, while recognizing that all the psycho-analytic psychologies contain much error and are in various ways very inadequate, we should nevertheless welcome their extension to the social field. For those of us who are not practising psycho-analysts are at a hopeless disadvantage when we challenge the psycho-analysts on their own ground of psycho-pathology ; whereas in the field of Social Psychology we may meet the analysts on common ground, with some hope of making effective intellectual contact, some hope of bridging, and even of closing, the gap that yawns between psychology and psycho-analysis, some hope of assimilating to the former whatever is true and new in the latter. Such closing of the gap would be a great boon to psychology ;

[1] Baltimore, 1934.

its continuing existence is an intellectual scandal of the first magnitude and worse than a scandal: the hostility between psychologists and psycho-analysts is seriously detrimental to all parties concerned, and brings all alike into disrepute with the general public.

Now, the only way to close this gap, or to diminish it, is the way of discussion between psycho-analysts and psychologists. Unfortunately the former are but little disposed to enter into such discussion. They, for the most part, require of the psychologist unconditional surrender without parley of any sort. The disciples of each psycho-analytical sect are quite sure that they alone see the truth, and that their prophet is the only true prophet.

We must seek to conciliate them by recognizing what virtues we can in their doctrines, and by gently insinuating possibilities of improvement.

In pursuance of that policy I repeat here and now, as my well-considered judgement, what I wrote of Professor S. Freud ten years ago in my *Outline of Abnormal Psychology*, namely: in my opinion Freud has, quite unquestionably, done more for the advancement of our understanding of human nature than any other man since Aristotle.[1]

[1] In order that there may be no mistake about my attitude to Professor Freud, I add that in my judgement he is a great man, both morally and intellectually; I esteem and admire him greatly.

THE PSYCHO-ANALYTIC DOCTRINES AN INTIMATE BLEND OF TRUTH AND ERROR

This judgement implies, of course, that there is much that is of value and relatively true in Freud's teaching. And yet I hold that every bit of such truth is mixed almost inextricably with error; or embedded in masses of obscure implications and highly questionable and misleading propositions. It is not so much that one cannot accept many of Freud's statements of fact; but rather that all his statements of fact are made in terms that imply unacceptable theories. Let me give one illustration out of a multitude. I accept without reserve the view that much mental activity is beyond the reach of our introspective efforts; and I have no serious objection to the description of such activities as *unconscious* (though I prefer to call them *subconscious*). But Freud and his disciples, most perversely as I think, have insisted on making an entity, *the Unconscious*, a quasi-personification of all subconscious activities. This, it may be said, is a mere *façon de parler*; and surely men of science should be able to understand one another in spite of variations of terminology. But the difficulty is much more serious than one of terminology only. Freud panders to every vice of popular speech and thinking; and, by doing so, effectively appeals to the lay public (in matters psychological the medical men are part of the lay public) and puts his scientific critics at a grave disadvantage. The Freudian points to undeniable evidence of some particular subconscious activity and says: Well then how can you deny *the Unconscious*? It is like the famous counsel's question: Have you left off beating your wife? I answer that the recognition of subconscious activities is of the first importance; but *the Unconscious* is a fraudulent entity that has gravely obstructed the path of progress. And much the same may be said of all the array of other quasi-personal entities, the *censor*, the *libido*, the *ego*, the *ego-ideal*, the *id*, &c., &c., with which Freud, indulging an unfortunate tendency of popular thinking, has cumbered the earth.[1]

DIFFICULTIES OF MAKING CONTACT WITH THE FREUDIANS

These popular but vicious modes of speaking and thinking add greatly to the difficulties of effective discussion between psycho-analysts and psychologists. The Freudians, it would seem, are for the most part incapable not only of thinking in any other terms than their own, but also of understanding anything written in other terms. I illustrate again. I have made many attempts to engage the master himself in discussion, in the form of an array of courteous and appreciative

[1] In a less degree only in virtue of his smaller following, the same is true of Dr. C. G. Jung.

criticisms of his teachings.[1] In only one instance have I succeeded; and the results were none too gratifying. Only in one of his publications has he taken notice of my work; but this, as it happens, concerns that problem of fundamental importance, the problem of suggestion. In my Social Psychology (of 1908) I put forward briefly a theory of suggestion, which was, as I believe (looking back on it now with the relative detachment that comes with the lapse of a quarter of a century) new, comprehensive, and substantially true. I pointed out that every instance of successful suggestion involves the release, or the setting to work in the subject, of some conative energy; and the two essential problems of suggestion are: (1) What is the nature and source of that conative energy or impulse? (2) How is it released and directed? Now on other grounds

[1] Besides the chapters of my *Outline of Abnormal Psychology* (London and New York, 1927) I may point to the following articles:

Critical notice of *Totem and Taboo* in *Mind*, 1920.

'Professor Freud's Group Psychology and his Theory of Suggestion', in the volume of *Essays in Psychopathology*, dedicated to Morton Prince, Boston, 1924.

'A Great Advance of the Freudian Psychology', *Journal of Abnormal and Social Psychology*, vol. xx. 1925.

'The Oedipus Complex, an Attempt to Estimate its Rôle and Importance', *Archives of Neurology and Psychiatry*, vol. 15, 1926.

All of these articles are reprinted as appendices to these lectures.

(having nothing to do with suggestion), grounds mainly of comparative psychology, I had found myself driven to postulate as a feature of the native endowment of the human species, an impulse to defer, to submit, to follow, to obey, a tendency or propensity of submission. There, I said, is the source of the conative energy evoked and operative in all successful suggestion ; and the art of suggesting, I said, is the art of setting that propensity into action, of evoking its impulse, and of directing it towards particular goals.

This theory I have defended and elaborated in later books and articles,[1] especially in my article 'A Note on Suggestion' of 1920.[2] Now, in his *Group Psychology*, Freud begins by recognizing the fundamental importance for all Social Psychology of the problem of suggestion. He remarks that he has ignored it for thirty years and that, on now coming back to it, he finds no advance has been made, no acceptable theory formulated. He goes on to survey the views of various writers. He makes a brief and very inadequate statement of my views, and having brushed aside my theory of suggestion, without examination, he proceeds to restate it as his own, mixing it wellnigh inextricably with a highly fanciful history of the supposed differentiation from the sex instinct in

[1] My *Group Mind*, *Outline of Psychology*, *Outline of Abnormal Psychology*, and *Energies of Men*.

[2] *Journal of Neurology and Psychopathology*, No. 1, vol. 1, 1920.

primitive man of that submissive propensity which he and I agree in postulating and in regarding as the source of the conative energy at work in all suggestion. Now I am sure that Professor Freud did not mean to steal my theory ; I feel sure that he is not aware of having done so. I am delighted that he should agree with me ; I would be still more pleased if he would acknowledge the fact of agreement.[1] I refer to this instance as illustrating the great difficulty in the way of fruitful discussion between psycho-analysts and psychologists.

[1] In his *Group Psychology* Freud refers specifically to my ' Note on Suggestion ' (loc. cit.) in which my theory is very explicitly restated. He refers to the article as though it were merely an attempt to define the proper usage of the word, an attempt which he seems to accept ; but since his remarks make it clear that he has read the article, I cannot see that he can be acquitted of the venial error of subconscious plagiarism. The incident illustrates one drawback of my now abandoned policy of modesty, of abstention from all claims of priority and independence. If my article had been entitled ' A New Theory of Suggestion ', Freud could hardly have fallen into this error.

CHAPTER II

VARIOUS PSYCHO-ANALYTIC EXCURSIONS INTO THE FIELD OF SOCIAL PSYCHOLOGY

In the first lecture of this short series I frittered away your time while you patiently heard me dwell on the great importance and the great difficulty of bringing together psycho-analysts and psychologists on the common ground of Social Psychology. If that first lecture was not very wide of the mark, it follows that, when any psycho-analyst enters the field of Social Psychology with friendly gestures towards his fellow-workers in that field, and proceeds to discuss social problems with an air of sweet reasonableness and gentle persuasiveness, it behoves us to welcome him and to examine his views in the most cordial spirit. Happily such a one is not far to seek. Such a one is our distinguished colleague, Professor J. C. Flügel.

PROFESSOR FLÜGEL'S EXCURSIONS

Professor Flügel may, I think, be described as a fairly orthodox Freudian, who in various books and articles has applied the doctrines of his school to social problems with candour and vigour. But, more than that, he is almost alone among psycho-analysts in that he shows himself well acquainted with, and even appreciative of, psychological theories other than those of his own school. He appears indeed to be not altogether beyond the reach of appeals to reason and evidence ; to be, in fact, a Freudian, possibly the only Freudian, capable of entering into fruitful controversy with psychologists.[1]

This outstanding position among the Freudians Flügel owes, no doubt, in part to a constitutional balance which gives a persuasiveness to all his writings ; but, since the privilege of introducing him to Psychology was mine, I like to think that it is due, in part, also to the fact that, whereas most other Freudians have been medical men who have plunged into psycho-analysis without any prior acquaintance with psychology, Flügel succumbed to the seductions of the Master when already a well-equipped psychologist ; a fact which, of itself, gives his discussions a stronger claim to careful consideration than those of his fellow disciples.

Flügel, then, may well be destined to become the path of conduction through which psychology may assimilate what is sound in the Freudian contribution, and to play the rôle of mediator by whom the Freudian disciples may be led over into

[1] The width and relative catholicity of Flügel's interests, as well as his sound learning and judgement, are displayed in his recent historical sketch, *One Hundred Years of Psychology*. London, 1933.

the fold of a psychology thus enlarged, enlightened, and reformed. We turn with high hopes to his recent volume, wholly devoted to the discussion of social problems.[1] The longest essay in the book is entitled 'Sexual and Social Sentiments'. It sets out by defining a fundamental question at issue between psycho-analysis and psychology; and seems to propose a judicial examination of it; namely—Are all the social forces, all the motives of social activity, so many diverse modes of operation of the sex instinct, so many manifestations of *libido*? Or can some of them be traced to inborn conative dispositions distinct from that of sex?

PROFESSOR FLÜGEL'S VIRTUES

Flügel's statement of this most fundamental issue presents several significant and welcome features. First, his use of the word 'sentiment', in the sense in which I have long striven to give it currency, is a considerable concession to psychology on the part of a Freudian; it is a welcome sign of a mind not wholly closed to non-Freudian influences.[2]

[1] *Men and their Motives.* London, 1934.

[2] That my theory of the sentiments must be one of the foundation stones of social psychology is an opinion not confined to myself alone; but slowly gaining ground, e.g., Professor Malinowski in an essay of 1930 ('Parenthood the Basis of Social Structure', in the volume *The New Generation*) refers to it as 'the most important contribution to modern

Secondly, in this, as in the other essays of the volume, Flügel shows himself to be a thoroughly *hormic* psychologist; that is to say, although so largely influenced by Freud, he makes no use of those two false foundation-stones of the Freudian system, namely, 'the pleasure principle' and 'the reality principle'. Rather, he is everywhere consciously concerned with the problem of tracing all motives, all desires, all impulsions or conations, to their instinctive sources; he explicitly asserts the fundamental importance of 'an exact determination of the sources of the conative (instinctual) energy engaged in every activity'.

Thirdly, Flügel recognizes that little has been surely established in the way of answers to the problem thus defined: he writes of 'the present vast uncertainty concerning the nature and interrelations of the instinctual energies'; a refreshing admission that the dogma of the *libido* is not all-sufficient.

Fourthly, Flügel, in this essay as in others, writes of 'really social tendencies', and of 'the gregarious and social tendencies with their resulting inhibitions embodied in that moral factor of the human mind which psycho-analysts have termed the super-ego'; he writes also of 'the co-operation of sexual and social instincts'.

Fifthly, Flügel's use of the word 'conation' in

psychology and social science'; and even Dr. Seligman who inclines to regard Freudian psycho-analysis as alone of any value, admits that the theory of the sentiments may be useful.

the sense in which it is now pretty well established among British psychologists is a very favourable sign. German psychology (including psycho-analysis) has been gravely hampered by the lack of any satisfactory equivalent for this word.[1]

Sixthly, Flügel (in this unlike most Freudians, who use the word 'sexual' with a reckless extension of meaning that deprives it of all value and makes all attempt at discussion with them as unsatisfactory as shadow-boxing, and who justify their usage, if at all, only by protesting that they are but following the example of Freud himself) offers us a perfectly satisfactory definition of the word 'sexual'.[2]

[1] The same may, I think, be said of French psychology. The German *Trieb* is, I suppose, the nearest to an equivalent. American psychologists, still dominated by the prestige of the Germans, suffer in the same way. The word 'drive', now freely used even by the 'behaviourists', is a translation of the German *Trieb*; but whereas the German word commonly implies the teleological or goal-seeking nature of the activity, the American 'drive' is commonly meant to be compatible in meaning with a strictly mechanistic view.

[2] 'It may be well to say a word about the meaning of the terms "sexual" and "social" as they will be used here. . . . By "sexual" (as applied to psychological material) we mean those mental processes which tend specificially to lead up to, and (ultimately) to accompany, the reproductive act or such substitutive acts as may give gratification of a kind that is usually associated with this act. Though narrower than the meaning usually given to "sexual" by psycho-analytic writers, such a view of the sexual still has a wide range, including the phenomena of courtship and romantic love upon the one

PROFESSOR FLÜGEL'S ERRORS AND DEFECTS

Flügel, in manifesting in his opening pages all these signs of grace, and, especially, in defining

hand and auto-eroticism and the perversions on the other.' This is excellent. But in defining the 'social' in the following sentence Flügel shows how difficult it is for one who has once accepted the yoke to avoid the vices of Freudian thinking. 'We may then go on to designate as "social" the mental processes, other than sexual, which tend to foster and accompany harmonious co-operation between the individuals of groups other than those directly determined by family relationship.' Why except the family groups? Clearly, because any mental process connected with family life is for the Freudian *ipso facto* sexual. He goes on: 'The "social" in this sense obviously covers a wide field. It embraces for instance that need for, and pleasure in, the presence of our fellows, together with the sensitivity to their opinion, which has been so largely emphasized by writers on Social Psychology. But it also includes conceptual factors such as love for and pride in a social group as distinct from the individuals composing it; factors which, as has often been pointed out, are of the very first importance for the higher forms of social conduct.' Here Flügel is clearly setting the stage for a friendly bout between the social psychology of Freud and that of McDougall. For the two topics specifically mentioned are the topics *par excellence* of my *Introduction to Social Psychology* and of my *Group Mind* respectively. The principal undertaking of the former book was to show how and why the individual becomes sensitive and responsive to the opinion of his fellows; that of the second, to show how and why participation in the life of the group is an essential presupposition of all 'higher forms of social conduct', in spite of the fact that every other social psychologist had represented such participation as invariably detrimental and degrading to the individual.

clearly and emphatically this fundamental question at issue between Psycho-analysis and Psychology, namely, the question of the single or multiple source of the conative energies that sustain all our social activities, raises high our hope that he will boldly face this question, striving for an unbiased decision. But such hope is quickly disappointed. For Flügel, having stated this very fundamental question at issue between psycho-analysis and psychology, makes not the feeblest attempt to examine it ; rather, he proceeds forthwith to elaborate in detail the fundamental doctrine of Freud's social psychology, namely, that all social relations are sexual.

It is true that he first rejects the rival view ; but assigns only the following most inadequate grounds for doing so. First, social motives, he says, often 'appear delicately interwoven with sexual motives . . . as in the promiscuous sexual gratifications of the ball-room, the sexual preoccupations of the *flaneur* and *boulevardier*, the "smutty" stories of the smoke-room and the scandal-mongering of the drawing room : an argument of a kind only too common in Freudian writings. Explicated it runs : the sex-impulse is unmistakably at work in a certain proportion of social activities, therefore all social activities are wholly sexual. What one here, as so often, complains of is, not that the argument is inconclusive, but that it affords no faintest presumption in favour of the view in support of which it is advanced: it is utterly and wholly lacking in logical cogency. It is as though Freud had laid an absolute tabu upon all logical or coherent reasoning, a tabu which works like a charm on all his disciples.

Secondly (and this is the only other ground adduced for the summary dismissal of the a-Freudian view), Freud is cited as having found two arguments against the hypothesis of a primary gregarious tendency in the human species: (*a*) every young child is frightened rather than pleased when he sees a stranger; (*b*) when at a later age any young person shows an inclination for the company of his fellows, this 'can be shown' to be a derivative from the 'Oedipus complex'. The argument again is of such logical disreputability as no intelligent person, other than a Freudian, would put forward. For suppose that, by a great effort of self-deception, we granted the two assertions (*a*) and (*b*); even then the conclusion drawn does not follow from those premises; there is implied an utterly untenable major premise, namely: every social activity springs from either the sexual or the alleged gregarious instinct alone.

Flügel reveals in the next sentence what seems to be the true ground of his total abandonment of the important task on which he seemed in his opening paragraph to have embarked: a review of the arguments for and against Freud's doctrine, he says, 'would probably necessitate a consideration of the whole *libido* concept, *itself a very formidable task*'. Precisely, any fundamental examination of Freud's doctrines is too formidable a task for any Freudian. To cast a sceptical glance upon the universal efficacy of the *libido* would be to lay sacrilegious hands on the ark of the covenant. The very few who have had the courage to undertake such examination have, in consequence, come out of the fold (or been cast out). One can remain in the fold only at the cost of observing strictly two tabus, the tabu on logic, and the tabu upon all critical examination of Freud's fundamental assumptions.

Flügel, having made this disappointing start, proceeds to discuss a number of problems which inevitably are raised by the assumption which is made the basis of Freud's Social Psychology. But the first and most urgent of these he ignores: namely—If all social tendencies are 'aim-inhibited' forms of the sex-impulse, by what force or forces are the sensual aims of the latter inhibited? In Freud's own account of the primal horde (in his *Group Psychology*), the thick stick wielded by the 'horde father' is the great instrument of such inhibition; but we are not told how the thick stick works primarily upon the mentality of its victims.

Quis custodes custodiet? What force is sufficiently powerful to inhibit the all-powerful *libido*? And how does the thick stick of the horde-father evoke and direct this super-force? It may seem natural and plausible enough to answer this question by invoking fear, the great universal inhibitor in men and animals. But that sane and simple answer is not open to Freud, because he has never yet recognized fear as an independent and primary impulse or instinctive mode of emotional conative reaction. He has, rather, indulged in a variety of tortuous efforts to exhibit fear as one mode of operation of the *libido*.

It is true that, since the date of publication of his *Group Psychology*, Freud has discovered or invented 'the self-preservative instinct'. But at that date one was left to suppose that the thick stick succeeded in paralysing or inhibiting the sensual aims of the sexual instinct by evoking that most dubious dynamic entity, 'the reality-principle'. Or, since in a later work Freud equates (strangely enough) 'the pleasure-principle' with the perception of pain,[1] it is open to any disciple to find in the pleasure-principle the answer to this fundamental problem so scandalously left unanswered by Freud. But, seriously speaking, this is only one of a series of great pseudo-problems gratuitously created by acceptance of Freud's hasty fundamental assumptions. I have later to point out that the advances of psycho-analysis largely consist in the throwing overboard of these pseudo-problems, one every few years, by the master-hand itself.

[1] *The Ego and the Id*, p. 66. 'The *id* guided by the pleasure-principle, that is, by the perception of pain. . . .'

FLÜGEL ON COMPETITION BETWEEN SEXUAL AND SOCIAL ACTIVITIES

The next problem to be defined by Flügel may be stated as follows : From the Freudian assumption that all social activities (other than the explicitly sexual) are sustained by aim-inhibited *libido* (or energy of the sex instinct) it clearly follows (unless it be assumed that each organism's supply of *libido* is unlimited) that in any given community there must obtain an inverse correlation between sexual and social activities ; the more of the *libido* is aim-inhibited and manifested as social activities, the less remains for directly sexual expression ; and conversely, the more of the *libido* finds directly sexual expression, the less the quantity left over for other social activities. Flügel does not hesitate to write down this deduction as a truth [1] : 'there exists,' he says, 'a certain antagonism between the manifestations of sexuality and those of sociality '. And the rest of the essay is largely concerned with the attempt to give colour to this assertion, an assertion which, on the face of it, is so flagrantly at variance with the facts.

Flügel, in support of the assertion, is content to adduce such facts as that the man absorbed in family interests (and, of course, to a Freudian

[1] A common Freudian practice—to deduce facts from theories.

every activity connected in any way with any family is explicitly sexual) gives little attention to other social activities (a simple case of the universal law of reciprocal limitation of interests). But, in a question of this sort, the more decisive evidence is provided by the extremer instances. We must look to the evidences afforded by the ascetic celibates on the one hand and by the libertines and free-livers on the other. The ascetics are the more significant by reason of the admitted fact that many of them are persons in whom the sex impulse is strong, though strongly inhibited. Do we, then, invariably find them distinguished by the extent of their social activities ? Do we not rather find them standing immovable on one leg, or otherwise withdrawn from social life, hermits and anchorites hiding in caves or deserts, or in retreat in monasteries, or on remote mountains (cp. the Trappist monks as an extreme instance), dwellers in asylums of many kinds ? Consider the other extreme of the scale, the sexual free-livers, the Casanovas, the Don Juans, the Falstaffs, the various royal libertines from Julius Caesar and Nero to Henry the Eighth, Charles the Second and George the Fourth. Are they invariably or commonly recluses ? Are they not rather in almost all cases eminently and actively social ?

Again, compare the sexually uninhibited communities, such as those of the Trobriand Islands, of Tahiti and of Hawaii, with the morosely unsociable Red Skins or the puritan communities of old New England.[1]

[1] Dr. G. D. Unwin (*Sex and Culture*, London, 1934) has recently adduced a mass of evidence which seems to establish a positive correlation between the levels of culture attained by various communities and the degree of social inhibition of sex activities. Dr. Flügel may wish to adduce this as new empirical evidence in support of his deduction. But level of culture is by no means identical with, or highly correlated with, extent and degree of social activities, either in individuals or communities. There are social activities which are trivial, unproductive and positively prejudicial so far as progress of culture is concerned. It is the more serious and strenuous forms of social activity which alone promote culture. One might cite dancing to jazz bands as a typical instance of social activity of the former kind, one highly compatible with lack of all sexual restraint: the cultivation of serious drama or music as an instance of the other kind, the kind which can thrive only in a society where restraint is imposed and practised. Dr. Unwin's evidence of the correlation of high culture with sexual restraint (to which I myself had pointed in an essay of 1924: 'Should all Tabus be Abolished?' in the volume *Sex in Civilization*) does bear out the reality and importance of *sublimation*. And the principle of sublimation, though not perhaps discovered and formulated absolutely *de novo* by Freud, is one the rôle and importance of which he more than any other has brought to light. This is only one of many services of Freud which I freely recognize. But the recognition of the many important contributions he has made should not be permitted to paralyse our intellects and suspend our critical powers in relation to his every assumption. Unfortunately this is one of the ways in which the human mind is very apt to be led into error; although it is not formally recognized by logicians as a type of fallacious thinking. Instances abound in modern science. Many years ago I

FLÜGEL ON JEALOUSY AND SOCIAL ACTIVITIES

An examination of all the pseudo-problems raised by the acceptance of the fundamental dogma of Freudian social psychology (namely, that all social activities derive from sex and are sustained by the *libido*) is impossible in these few lectures. I mention in this connexion only one other, one to which Flügel devotes a whole chapter of the volume under examination, namely, jealousy and its relation to social activity.

All social activities (other than the explicitly sexual) are the expression of aim-inhibited libido, i.e. of energy derived from the sex instinct but diverted into channels of expression other than the explicitly sexual : that is the fundamental thesis of Freudian social psychology. Further, as Flügel puts it, all 'sexual inhibitions ultimately depend indirectly

drew attention to one such in the history of theories of colour-vision : Ewald Hering having criticized effectively certain of Helmholtz's additions to Thomas Young's theory, and having described certain novel phenomena, gained a prestige in this sphere which led almost all the physiologists and psychologists of Germany, England and America to accept his theory in place of Young's, in spite of the fact that it involved various obscure and, indeed, manifestly untenable assumptions. The story of Weissmann's success in leading general repudiation of the Lamarckian principle in the same countries is a second great incident of the same kind. While the story of the spread of the Freudian doctrines is a third great instance, which will probably live in history as the most notable of the three.

upon jealousy'. This second proposition also is fundamental in the Freudian creed; and it has the considerable advantage of being, in part, true.

In the Freudian scheme, the inhibition of the sexual aims of the young men by the thick stick of the horde-father is the prototype of all sexual inhibitions in all ages and all cultures; and the thick stick is, of course, the instrument of the horde-father's sex-jealousy. Hence, it follows that the more effectively and fiercely sex-jealousy operates in any community, the more must social activities flourish; and conversely, without jealousy, no sociality; and the less intensely jealousy is felt and manifested, the feebler must be all social activities other than the explicitly sexual.

Is this plain deduction from the two premises consistent with empirical facts? Is it not, rather, in conflict with a wealth of facts? Purdah and the harem are two forms of strongly expressed and institutionalized sex-jealousy; yet they are notoriously enemies of social activities. They are always the first objects of attack by social reformers who seek to develop the social life and activities of communities thus bound and retarded.

The facts of this order (revealing the anti-social influence of excessive sex-jealousy) are so many and so obvious that the candid Flügel cannot ignore them. He then gets himself tied up in the following tangle: All social activity expresses aim-inhibited sex-energy. Jealousy is the ultimate ground of all such aim-inhibition, and is therefore the essential, the indispensable ground of all social activity; and, since all social activity is begotten out of *libido* by jealousy, it follows that jealousy is the essential ground of the antagonism between sexual and social sentiments alleged and expounded at length by Flügel. Nevertheless, 'Sociality implies a limitation of jealousy' and 'this influence (jealousy) is therefore opposed to the antagonism between sexual and social tendencies from which we set out'.[1]

[1] I have frequently observed that when a writer's thinking becomes confused and self-contradictory, his language becomes wellnigh unintelligible. I cite the following passage from the last page of Flügel's essay on 'Sexual and Social Sentiments' as an interesting illustrative specimen. 'Sociality implies a limitation of jealousy and of the right of exclusive possession over children or sexual partner, whereas the family is to a large extent founded on the *patria potestas*. Since sexual inhibitions also ultimately depend indirectly upon jealousy, there is here at work an influence which tends to produce a positive correspondence between sexual freedom and the preponderating influence of larger social groups (and a negative correspondence between sexual freedom and preponderating influence of the family. [This influence is therefore opposed to the antagonism between sexual and social tendencies from which we set out.]' The function of the square brackets (which occur in Flügel's text) seems to be to soften in some measure the violence of the contradiction.

JEALOUSY THE ROOT OF ALL SOCIALITY MUST BE ABOLISHED IN THE INTERESTS OF INCREASE OF SOCIALITY

Here are opposite effects deduced from one and the same cause ; but Flügel, like all true Freudians, is so well accustomed to this operation, that the paradox he reaches gives him no pause. Not only is he blind to this insoluble paradox ; but also he forthwith proceeds (in the following essay) to develop at length an argument for the abolition of jealousy in the interests of greater sociality [1] ; totally oblivious of the fact that in the preceding essay he has faithfully upheld the doctrine that jealousy is the indispensable root of all sociality and of all society.[2]

[1] In the former essay he has sagely forecast the casting out of all jealousy and the coming of a happy age of promiscuity, and added : 'if it (the abolition of jealousy) is accomplished, it seems clear that the antagonism between the claims of sex and of society will be very much reduced'. He might safely have gone further in this process of deduction from Freudian dogmas ; he might with impeccable logic have foreseen that the abolition of jealousy would totally abolish the antagonism between the claims of sex and of society ; for, since by the hypothesis, jealousy is the essential ground of all social life, to abolish it would be to abolish society itself.

[2] Since my readers may find it difficult to believe that I am faithfully representing the divagations of so estimable a Freudian, I must cite in Flügel's own words one of the many passages in which he deprecates or roundly condemns as destructive of society that very factor, jealousy, which he has so copiously expounded as the living mainspring of all social life. 'Jealousy is, therefore, a true and natural sanction of

Perhaps it would be unfair to cite all this floundering about between two opposite views of jealousy and its social influence as an example of the intellectual wreckage which seems to be the price paid for admission into the Freudian horde. It may be that this particular instance of logical myopia (or is it anopia ?) is wholly due to moral fervour. We all know how moral enthusiasm may pervert our intellectual operations. And Flügel writes as a fervent exponent (strictly in theory, of course) of the sex-morals of the Russell-Wells school ; that is to say, the morals of that school of reformers who roundly condemn all jealousy and who, without deprecating marriage altogether (for, after all, even the most faded wife may have her uses as secretary or housekeeper, provided that she has been taught to see the beauty of the new morality), would restrict marital

the patriarchal system [and of the family], and is looked upon as reasonable and laudable by those to whom this system [the family system] seems the keystone of social life and civilization. It is, on the other hand, largely incompatible with a system of liberty, equality, and fraternity, in which every individual has some right to the free bestowal of his or her affection and in which this right is regarded as of greater importance than the right of property. Jealousy is naturally and inevitably disruptive of this latter system, which cannot be so tolerant of exclusive privileges over individuals or over property. *Quite rightly*, therefore, the upholders of this system condemn jealousy, *as an emotion which is harmful to society* and which inflicts unnecessary suffering and frustation.' And that he (Flügel) is of the latter party he leaves no room for doubt.

fidelity to week-days, while reserving week-ends and holidays for other peoples' spouses or for the casual attractive stranger.

FLÜGEL AND THE OEDIPUS COMPLEX

Would that I could report the other essays of this stimulating volume as redressing by their strict logicality the balance between reason and loyalty to Freud! All of them contain much ingenious reasoning from the same fixed premises. The most interesting perhaps is the one on the character of Henry VIII. Real light is thrown, I think, on this problem; especially in pointing out that Henry seems to have had a persistently bad conscience about his marriage with Catherine of Aragon, on the ground that she was his brother's widow. But the application of this fact (if fact it be) is overdriven; and many assumptions are made and used as premises which, at the best, are mere probabilities. For example, it is assumed that Henry, when, as a boy of ten years, he played a part in the official reception of his brother's bride, promptly (according to the Tristram tradition) fell in love with her and suffered pangs of jealousy towards his brother. Yet, when his brother dies and it is proposed to Henry that he shall marry the widow, he allows three years to elapse before complying. And when, in accordance with his dying father's wish, 'the marriage was indeed hurried forward with almost indecent haste', a natural attraction towards the bride, previously postulated, is given no credit ; rather, the motives of Henry's action are found in ' tendencies emanating from the Oedipus complex ', and in these tendencies alone. This is typical of the procedure throughout this essay. The author is never satisfied with any assignment of motivation, however sexual, that does not give him scope for the display of subtilty (at whatever cost of logic). Again and again, with superfluity of subtilty, he drags in the Oedipus complex (fourteen times in all in this one essay) as the true source of motivation. It is, in short, his King Charles's head.

That Flügel should show this excess of regard for the Oedipus complex is a curious manifestation, itself in need of explanation. As a retort to his cavalier treatment of ' the herd instinct ', I am tempted to invoke the influence of that much-disputed entity. Clearly, this peculiarity cannot be explained as determined merely by loyalty to his master or by submission to his authority. For, as I have pointed out in some detail as long ago as 1925, Freud himself has ceased to regard the Oedipus complex as present in the mental structure of healthy adults in general, and, in doing so, has undermined the evidence for its formation in all or most infants ; for the only alleged evidence of its formation in all infants was (in its hey-day) its alleged manifestations in all adults.[1]

But perhaps, after all, this continuing devotion

[1] Cp. Appendix IV.

to the Oedipus complex is only an instance of 'delayed reaction': for I notice that in general, when Professor Freud introduces one of his big changes of doctrine, an interval of about ten years elapses before his disciples seem to be duly converted to the improvement, or even to become aware of it.

I cannot pass on without a word on a very delicate topic. Flügel in his essay on sexual and social sentiments professes to be investigating the rival claims of Freud and of other social psychologists to offer satisfactory explanations of the leading phenomena of social life. His language makes it clear that, under the latter head, he has in view chiefly myself. But whereas, in setting forth Freud's views, he makes specific reference to his works at least a dozen times, the essay contains not one specific reference to any work of mine. And, while Freud's name occurs in this one essay thirty-two times, mine occurs only five times. Now this is not only evidence of bias, which was to be expected; but is, I submit, hardly fair to me. I am made in a vague general way responsible for all and any views which any non-Freudian social psychologists have put forward; while Freud is held responsible for his own views only. And, while I get no credit for any sound contributions I may have made, I have to carry the opprobrium for all the errors of other non-Freudian social psychologists.

OTHER EXCURSIONS ON THE COMMON GROUND

I turn from Professor Flügel's highly readable and intriguing pages to other very recent excursions of psycho-analysts into the field of Social Psychology. And I go no further afield than the last number of the *British Journal of Medical Psychology* (vol. XX. Part I): for that number is mainly occupied with such excursions: and I wish to avoid the retort that I am dealing with out-of-date and discarded views.

Let us note first that Dr. E. Miller (in his presidential address to the Medical Section of the British Psychological Society) claiming and manifesting advantages similar to those enjoyed by Flügel in approaching psycho-analysis, displays a healthy scepticism, indulges in some refreshing criticisms, and concludes thus: 'The major causes for discontent in psycho-pathology lie therefore in the field of neurological and psychological interpretation, in the complexity of psychological theories [he means theories of the psycho-analysts] which have wandered unnecessarily from biological principles, and lastly in erroneous social interpretations.' Surely, a pretty comprehensive indictment!

In addition to this sweeping general criticism, the one serious contribution towards reform made in this address by Dr. Miller is the pointing out of the error of Freud's pleasure-principle, the error which makes this principle pervade the *id* and dominate the infant ; whereas, in truth, the hedonic principle begins to play a rôle of some importance only in the highly sophisticated adult. But (as I pointed out in my article, 'A Great Advance of the Freudian Psychology '[1]) Freud himself, more than a decade ago, had partially revoked this error. Yet more recently he seems to have relapsed somewhat, if we may judge by such recent expressions as the following : 'The pleasure-principle, which exerts undisputed sway over the processes in the *id* '.

THE MOTIVATION OF ACQUISITIVE BEHAVIOUR

A large part of the number is occupied by 'A Symposium on Property and Possessiveness ', which brings psycho-analysts and social psychologists together on this common ground in an endeavour to solve the problem of the motives at work in acquisitive behaviour. And, just as in Flügel's discussion of 'Sexual and Social Sentiments ', the problem posed is whether all the behaviour in question derives in one way or another from the sex instinct or from some other one alleged instinct. In Flügel's discussion the only rival considered is the alleged herd-instinct ; in this case the solitary rival is the alleged acquisitive instinct. All the symposiasts alike, both psycho-analysts and psychologists, are much con-

[1] *Journal of Abnormal and Social Psychology*, vol. xx. 1925, reprinted in this volume as Appendix III.

cerned to repudiate a purely mythical psychologist who is supposed to have put forward the latter view. In this they have less justification than Flügel; for he could point, if not to a psychologist, at least to a surgeon [1] who had expounded, with whimsical brilliance, the obviously mistaken doctrine of the motivation of all social activity by the herd instinct alone. Of course our symposiasts have no difficulty in showing that the motivation of economic or acquisitive behaviour is in general highly complex. And, equally of course, the assumption (against which their arguments are directed)—either the sex instinct or some other one instinct—is absurd.

DR. SUTTIE ON ACQUISITIVE BEHAVIOUR

Dr. J. D. Suttie leads off with some remarks about non-rational factors in 'economic' behaviour, in the course of which, while effectively criticizing the popular assumption that acquisitive behaviour alone is rational, he reveals an implicit belief that some forms of behaviour are, or may be, purely rational, in the sense of owing nothing to *desire* or conation, and everything to reason. Misled by Freud's false 'reality principle', he has not fully realized the force of David Hume's famous remark that 'reason is and ought to be the slave of the passions'.[2] He proceeds to apply

[1] Mr. Wilfred Trotter.

[2] E.g. he suggests that 'our own economic system is not the logical expression of utilitarian motives, and that our economic

to the problem of economic motivation his own version of the Freudian thesis that all social behaviour is sexually motivated.

Dr. Suttie sees the motive of all acquisitive behaviour in 'separation-anxiety'. 'It is not need or greed which drives the individualists and communists into collision, but the separation-anxiety arising from love-privation in early childhood': it is 'a form of the universal love quest that dominates human life from the cradle to the grave'; . . . 'personal property is a means of overcoming the separation-anxiety. . . . Patrimony represents psychologically, or is a means of recapturing, or is a substitute for, the nurtural mother.'

This seems clear and explicit enough: the infant's *libido*, 'fixated' on the mother, seeks a substitute for her in property; and the activities thus directly sustained by the sex-impulse are those we call 'economic'. But on the next page, in the chameleonic fashion with which readers of Freudian literature are only too familiar, Dr. Suttie jumps without warning to a different theory

behaviour has neither the *uniformity of instinct* nor the practical and rational character one would expect to proceed from motives of self-interest, foresight, and reality-thinking generally'. On which one is tempted to comment that 'uniformity of instinct' coming from a Freudian is good; for the infinite variety of behaviour springing from one instinct is one of the characteristic doctrines of the school.

of economic motivation and derives it from the 'instincts of self-preservation'.[1]

Nevertheless, he quickly comes back to his first love, his own peculiar version of King Charles's head, 'separation-anxiety'; for, though he recognizes tendencies to excel, to seek distinction, to be of consequence, to be aggressive, to be competitive, and also the desire of power, all these (and I suppose all other motives which may enter into economic activity, such as mere hunger and thirst, or a desire to provide for one's children's future or to pay one's debts), all these desires are for him but protean forms of 'separation-anxiety'. Thus not money but weaning becomes the root of all evil. And finally, all these tendencies are transmuted, in a closing paragraph, into one great economic motive, the desire 'to have what other people need'.[2] The implied prescription for all our ills seems to be: bottle-feeding for all, begun

[1] Pretty obviously without himself being aware that he is propounding a second and quite different solution of the one problem. In this he illustrates a common Freudian trait; one which arises naturally enough from the practice of putting forward the wildest speculative guesses in full confidence that they will never be brought up sharply against facts or required to fit into any well-established and logically coherent scheme.

[2] No reason for this final transformation scene is offered, and the motivation of it is not obvious. It seems to be effected in obedience to a general principle accepted as an injunction by most Freudians, though not I believe explicitly asserted by Freud himself; namely, Be as cynical as you can!

at birth and continued until death or old age shall render us harmless.

DR. ISAACS DISPLAYS THE ARDOUR OF A CONVERT

Dr. Susan Isaacs recognizes 'the possessive impulse'; but regards it as highly complex, as compounded, in fact, of many impulses, impulses of rivalry, of guilt, of love and of hate, and the desire of power. She, even more than the other symposiasts, is concerned to refute the mythical defender of an instinct of acquisition as the sole inspirer of all economic activity. Her zeal in this cause carries her to an excess in the opposite direction; she asserts that desire to possess is always a triangular relation between at least two people and the thing in question, and that 'few objects, other than food when hungry, have an absolute and intrinsic value to little children, independent of what other children are having or wanting'.[1]

Having made her point (and overdriven it in true Freudian fashion) Dr. Isaacs must show herself to be of the true faith. She seems to bethink herself: Prithee, come up! I have mentioned neither faeces nor penes, nor castration nor anal-eroticism, nor any other of the tasty morsels which

[1] I am forcibly reminded of 'Jacko', a tattered remnant of fur (once a furry monkey-doll) tenderly treasured by one of my own household long after the date when every other member desired to commit him to the dust-bin. An instance surely of a not uncommon type of absolute valuation by a child of an object for its own sake!

readers of psycho-analytic stuff are accustomed to expect. Some ignoramus will be taking me for a mere squeamish psychologist. And what will they think of me in Wimpole Street ? So she lets herself go for the space of one page in a fine Freudian frenzy : 'The ultimate situation from which the wish to own arises is that of the infant at the breast.' She makes a perfectly gratuitous complimentary reference to the work of Dr. Melanie Klein (perhaps the most ultra-Freudian of all Freudians) and winds up with : 'Sweets are craved instead of the breast because the person who gives them remains undamaged by the loss. Faeces, money and mechanical toys are feverishly sought instead of the penis, because these, if broken or ruined, can be thrown away and easily replaced. [Surely a grave failure fully to appreciate the sadistic component of the sex instincts !] The anal fixations represented in love of material possessions are thus strongly reinforced by displacement from the breast and the penis.' For all desired material objects 'are in the main a substitute for love' and, I suppose, 'feed his sacred flame'.

It is true that these last profundities are introduced with the words, 'It is possible to suggest that . . .' Well, of course, it is possible to suggest anything, if only one's audience be sufficiently suggestible. And in Freudian circles there would seem to be no limits to suggestibility. Shall I dare to add : especially among the women ?

I will add also a protest against an assumption which seems to be commonly implied among Freudians, the assumption, namely, that any wild hypothesis is likely to be true if only it be sufficiently nasty.

DR. FORSYTH GIVES THE *COUP DE GRÂCE* TO RELIGION

I will add a brief reference to one other very recent excursion of a Freudian into the field of Social Psychology; namely, the presidential address to the Psychiatric Section of the Royal Society of Medicine. Dr. David Forsyth may perhaps be regarded as a more faithful disciple of Freud than any of the others I have mentioned. Unfortunately a full report is not yet available.[1] The feature which drew much attention to the address was its claim that psychology has finally disposed of religion. Now I am not appearing on this occasion as a defender of religion. Here and now I am concerned rather with the defence

[1] I have to rely on the condensed report made in *The Times*. 'The reply made by psychology was that all processes of thinking were of two kinds: pleasure thinking and reality thinking. Pleasure thinking was well known under the name of 'imagination' and showed itself in dreams and daydreams. It was employed in all creative artistic work. Reality thinking enabled mental processes to influence the outer world: but pleasure thinking excluded the world of reality. . . . Modern civilization had no alternative but to make choice between religion and science. . . . The need was to cease applying pleasure thinking to the illusory aims of religion and to use it in advanced science.'

of the reputation of psychology. In that cause I venture to raise my voice in repudiation of Dr. Forsyth's claim to speak in the name of psychology. For what is the psychological argument with which he professes to deal a final blow to religion ? It is that all religion is the product of *imagination* ; and all imagining is the work of 'the pleasure-principle' ; and the pleasure-principle has nothing at all to do with reality ; all thinking about reality being the work of 'the reality-principle'. Hence all the objects of religious thinking, devotion and aspiration are unreal.[1]

I protest in the name of psychology. This distinction between two alleged all-powerful agencies, on the one hand the so-called 'pleasure-principle', and, on the other, the equally so-called 'reality-principle', is one of the flimsiest and least defensible of all Freud's many hasty assumptions, although it is one of those to which he still adheres. It is difficult to attack it, for the good reason that it remains merely a hasty assumption, little more than a form of words that carry no meaning—'a tale of little meaning though the words be strong'. I have already cited the adverse comment of Dr. Emanuel Miller, and have indicated that, in my opinion, in so far as pleasure-seeking governs our thinking, it is at a

[1] 'Psycho-analysis had severed its (religion's) very roots by showing that it belonged to the unreal and the fantasmal, and that it carried all the marks of a child mentality.' *The Times*, 12 November, 1934.

late and highly sophisticated stage of our development, and even then somewhat rarely.[1]

Whatever may be the exact role of pleasure in our cognitive or intellectual activities, it is quite certainly not that assigned by Dr. Forsyth. Yet in this groundless and indefensible, this utterly flimsy, assumption about the alleged pleasure-principle, he pretends to find a sufficient and final refutation of all religion.

Freud cannot repudiate his responsibility for this sort of thing. When he uses his immense prestige to disseminate as truths what are merely hasty and false assumptions (as he so frequently has done) he cannot justly complain if we hold him responsible for wild and reckless use made of his doctrines by his disciples.

And indeed Freud's own excursion into this particular field of social psychology, namely the psychology of religion, is hardly more respectable than the one we have just now noticed. Freud

[1] The total lack of clearness in Freud's own thinking about ' the pleasure-principle ' is illustrated by the passages cited and by my discussion of his partial revocation of this alleged active principle in Appendix III of this volume. The mere fact that in some passages Freud designates it alternatively as the pleasure-pain principle is highly significant. During more than two thousand years it has repeatedly been argued that ' the avoidance of pain ' is synonymous with ' the pursuit of pleasure '. But that identification remains an error still; however plausible the error may seem from a merely external or ' behaviourist ' point of view; and not even Freud's dictum can make it true. The reality-principle is even less clear, less plausible, less defensible.

uses similar arguments; his treatment differs merely in laying the emphasis differently.[1] In place of harping chiefly on 'the pleasure-principle', he asserts that psycho-analysis 'has traced the origin of religion to the helplessness of childhood, and its content to the persistence of the wishes and needs of childhood into maturity'. Hence, he argues, 'the truth of religion may be altogether disregarded'. Again: 'Religion is illusion and derives its strength from the fact that it falls in with our instinctual desires.'

The whole attack amounts to saying that man's nature is such as naturally leads to the development of religions, therefore religion is purely illusory. Exactly the same argument would with equal cogency lead to the conclusion that all science is purely illusory. The argument is one illustration among many of Freud's contempt for the laws of logic. The premises of the argument are roughly true, and we can fairly deduce from them the conclusion that the approximate universality of religious belief provides no sufficient guarantee of its truth. But Freud is not content with this valid and somewhat commonplace conclusion, which only a fanatic would reject. He leaps right over it to the conclusion that such belief is always and everywhere false. Truly, if it be true that Nature never makes leaps, Freud and his followers are most unnatural creatures.

[1] Cp. *The Future of an Illusion*, and *New Introductory Lectures on Psycho-analysis*. Chapter XXXV. London, 1933.

CHAPTER III

FREUD'S EXCURSIONS INTO SOCIAL PSYCHOLOGY AND THE CONSEQUENT PROGRESS OF THE PSYCHO-ANALYTIC THEORY OF HUMAN NATURE

HAVING been led thus to Freud's own excursions into the field of Social Psychology, I must devote the brief time remaining to indicate how these excursions are broadening and rectifying his views. For Freud himself recognizes that it is these excursions which are effecting the transformation of what began merely as a therapeutic method into a system of psychology, a psychology which claims to speak the fundamental and the final word in every field of social phenomena, in religion, education, economics, politics, and even in morals.

Let me say at once that I in no sense reproach Freud with these changes of view. Rather I regard the changes as evidence of his greatness, especially as, even in his old age, he continues to stride along far in advance of his followers, a true horde-leader, brandishing mightily the thick stick of office.

A lesser man having secured a respectable following for his doctrines, would be content to repeat them with minor variations and with damnable iteration ; as Adler repeats his scanty array of sweeping generalizations containing just enough of truth to give them plausibility for the lay public. Freud does not scruple to change his most fundamental propositions, and to pull them about in a way which, if they were the foundation-stones of a logically constructed system, would bring the whole structure tumbling upon this mighty Samson and his devoted followers.

It is true, of course, that if, in starting out to build a systematic account of human nature, you include a good few thumping big errors, you will have plenty of scope to advance by discovering and rejecting your errors. Freud gave himself this initial advantage in full measure.[1]

Let us notice some of the chief of these advances.

THE PASSING OF THE UNCONSCIOUS

The most startling of these reforms by repudiation is the revocation of ' the Unconscious ' as a part or region of the mind sharply distinguished from ' the Conscious ', and widely separated from the latter by a third whole region, ' The Fore-conscious '. ' The Unconscious ' surely has been commonly and rightly regarded as a chief pillar of the whole system. I don't know whether any

[1] For Freud's later views I rely largely on the authorized English translation of Freud's recent lectures entitled *New Introductory Lectures on Psycho-Analysis* (Hogarth Press, London, 1933), henceforth referred to as *New Lectures* or N.L.

one, either within or without the fold, has already pointed out that Freud himself has pulled this pillar to pieces. 'The Unconscious' used to comprise contents of two distinct kinds. First, all those parts of the structure of the mind which were debarred by repression from expressing themselves in consciousness. And, secondly, all unconscious activities. That is to say, under the one term, 'the Unconscious', certain parts of the total mental structure were confounded with certain modes of mental functioning or activity. Now we are told that 'the super-ego' (which is not in any sense part of that which is repressed, but is rather the great repressing agent)[1] 'can operate unconsciously in quite important situations, or which would be far more significant, that parts of both ego and super-ego themselves are unconscious. In both cases we should take account of the disturbing view that *the ego* (including the super-ego) *does not by any means completely coincide with the conscious, nor the repressed with the unconscious.*'

After this tremendous revelation, this revolution within the palace, this *coup d'état* made by the king himself, Freud says: 'Ladies and Gentlemen, I feel I must have a little breathing space.' And no wonder! Then, having taken breath for a space, he goes on to assert: 'Certainly, large portions of the ego and super-ego can

[1] *New Lectures*, p. 93. 'We can say that repression is the work of the super-ego.'

remain unconscious, are, in fact, normally unconscious . . . we are forced fundamentally to revise our attitude towards the problem of conscious and unconscious.' Ladies and Gentlemen, I demand a little breathing space, in which to throw up my hat and shout 'hurrah'! For this means progress. Freud goes on to revoke most of what was objectionable in his old Unconscious. He puts it in this way. The term 'the Unconscious' was formerly used to cover two very different things: first, as a term descriptive of certain mental activities; secondly, as a term descriptive of certain ill-defined parts of the total mental structure: or, in his own language, it was used not only as a term descriptive of a certain kind of mental activity, but also in the sense of a system, it was given 'a topographical or systematic meaning'.[1]

This double meaning of the term 'the Unconscious' was exactly the vice of it to which I for one have most strongly objected ever since I made acquaintance with it some thirty years ago, and even at an earlier date, in the pages of von Hartmann's celebrated treatise, 'The Philosophy of the Unconscious', which is pervaded by the same vice.

In the *New Lectures* we read: 'We will no longer use the word "unconscious" in the sense of a system, and to what we have hitherto called by that name we will give a better one . . . we

[1] *New Lectures*, p. 96.

will call it henceforward the "*id*"'. Again I shout—Hurrah! For this is progress.[1]

Yet the '*id*'! There is still confusion of the kind that is inevitable so long as Freud persists in the vicious practice of applying to mental functions his topographical method, a method which has a certain validity when, and only when, applied to mental structures. The *id* is defined most concisely as 'instinctual cathexes seeking discharge—that is all that the *id* contains.' Is, then, the *id* simply the sum of the instincts? On some pages it would seem so: for the *id* is unconscious, it is 'a cauldron of seething excitement'[2] and is the great reservoir of *libido*,[3] and in it 'the pleasure-principle exerts undisputed sway', and 'dominates all its processes'.[4] Further, 'the ego stands for reason and circumspection, while the *id* stands for the untamed passions . . . one might compare the relation of the ego to the *id* with that between a rider and his horse'. Here we are back at Plato's doctrine of Reason as the charioteer who guides the fierce unruly horses, the passions, which are the motive powers. Even

[1] Ibid. p. 97. I may be allowed to point out that for some decades I have been urging upon psychologists of all schools (without success) the necessity of distinguishing clearly between mental structure and mental functions, a distinction so utterly obscured by the terminology of wellnigh all schools. I rejoice therefore to see Freud at last accepting and insisting upon this distinction.

[2] *Ibid.* p. 98.

[3] *The Ego and the Id*, p. 38.

[4] *New Lectures*, p. 100.

the topographical separation of the *id* and the reason was at least as clear in Plato's teaching as in Freud's. For Plato put Reason in the head, and the *id* in the belly. Whereas Freud does not yet seem to know that the *id* corresponds roughly to the thalamic region of the brain and reason to the cortex.

But the doctrine of the *id*, *at present* is not so clear, so simple, as this. It is still a great tangle in which Freud lashes about like a great whale caught in a net of his own contriving. He says quite explicitly: 'Super-ego, ego and *id*, then, are the three realms, regions or provinces into which we divide the mental apparatus of the individual.'[1] This seems a pretty definite separation between ego and *id*; but it by no means corresponds with the distinction between the conscious and the unconscious. For, although the ego 'includes consciousness' (apparently all there is of consciousness) yet 'The ego is after all only part of the *id*'[2] (*New Lectures*, p. 102). Now

[1] *New Lectures*, p. 97.

[2] *Ibid*, p. 100. On this one page we are told both that 'instinctual cathexes seeking discharge, that in our view, is all that the *id* contains' and also that the ego is 'that part of the *id* which has been modified by its proximity to the external world', and 'repression is the work of the super-ego', which is a part of the ego, which is a part of the *id*. The following passage is also relevant at this point, relevant that is as revealing the vast confusion that still rules in Freud's mind, in spite of the great reform, the discarding of 'the Unconscious': 'I hope you will by now feel that in postulating

the super-ego is a 'function in the ego'; therefore the unconscious *id* includes within itself both ego and super-ego (which, two or three pages earlier in the chapter, have been emphatically separated from the *id* as distinct parts, 'realms, regions or provinces' of the mental apparatus) and, with them, the consciousness or conscious activities which they include.

I have said enough, I think, to show you that, although it was a great step to distinguish the two very different meanings which until recently had been confused together by Freud under the term 'the Unconscious', it is clear that the name '*id*', having been given to the topographical part thus separated out from the Unconscious, still covers a mass of gross confusion. I will not call it a hopeless confusion; for, if Professor Freud should have the strength to revise all this part of his doctrine once more, giving up once for all his obstinate inclination to confuse parts of mental structure with types of mental activity (a distinction whose importance he has now begun to realize), he will probably arrive at the tolerable conclusion that the name *id*, if it is to have any usefulness, must go back to the meaning which that great psychologist, Friedrich Nietzsche, gave to it, namely, the sum of the instinctive or innate dispositions.

the existence of a super-ego I have been describing a genuine structural entity, and have not been merely personifying an abstraction, such as conscience' (*Ibid.* p. 88).

CHANGES IN FREUD'S DOCTRINE OF *LIBIDO* AND THE INSTINCTS

A second great advance is Freud's revision of his account of instincts and his approach to the abandonment of the dogma of the *libido*. These two advances may be briefly reviewed together as one process. It has been a piecemeal gradual process.

It is roughly true that Freud set out to explain all our mental functionings in terms of the *libido*, the energy of the sex-instinct, alone. Thereupon he was confronted by the great facts of resistance, of repression, of conflict; all of which he has done so much to bring to light and to force upon the recognition of all but the most benighted psychologists. And the question before him was—What is the nature of the forces which resist, repress, and conflict with, the sex impulse? At first he made much play with such vague indefinable entities as the Conscious, the Censor, the Ego, the 'pleasure-principle' and the 'reality-principle'. Yet he would seem to have seen that the tremendous energy of the sex-impulse can be controlled, resisted, repressed, sublimated, only by the energies of other impulses which cannot be derived from the sex instinct itself.

Freud assumed, therefore, the existence of two fundamentally opposed instincts, 'two main instincts, or species or groups of instincts, corresponding to two great needs, hunger and love' and subserving 'two purposes, self-preservation and the preservation of the species' (*New Lectures*, p. 124). The former, the instinct of self-preservation, was identified with hunger and thirst. The latter was called the sex instinct or instincts, and to its energy Freud proposed to give the name *libido*. The infant is endowed with a number of simple impulses which later become fused to form the single sex instinct; but at a still later stage, the single instinct thus compounded proliferates or sheds off a number of tendencies which function more or less independently, though still activated by the common energy, the *libido*. What exactly is meant by saying that all these tendencies are activated by one energy or one kind of energy is not clear. For we know nothing of differences of kind among mental or neural or psychophysical energies.[1]

Nevertheless the word *libido* has served to justify the classing as sexual of a major part of all human activities; not only all sex activities such as they are well defined by Flügel in the passage cited above (p. 27, f. 2) but also all family activities; all behaviour that can be called social; all tender protective altruistic behaviour; all self-assertive, aggressive, angry or cruel behaviour (under the head of sadism); all submissive obedient, imitative and suggestible behaviour

[1] Unless it means that they all draw their energy from a common source, the one sex instinct; but this interpretation will hardly suffice to meet all Freud's demands upon the *libido*.

(under the head of masochism); all exploratory or curious behaviour; all modes of behaviour expressive of fear and of disgust.

Changes in this account of the instincts and the *libido* have consisted (*a*) in recognizing other instincts of the non-libidinous group; (*b*) in transferring to this group some of the functions of the libidinous group; (*c*) in giving a semi-independent or half-way status to some of the tendencies alleged to be derived from the sex instinct. Let us glance at the more important changes of these three kinds.

The first instincts to be added to the non-libidinous class were, I think, a group of ego-instincts. These have remained undefined, shrouded in mystery; and of late years they have tended to fade out of the picture. Freud seems to have found reason to transfer them to the libidinous group.

Far more revolutionary and disruptive has been the recognition of an aggressive instinct. The strange history of this step illustrates Freud's devious methods of progress. Freud did not look around him on his fellow-creatures, human and animal, to observe that everywhere, when impulse or desire is obstructed, aggressive behaviour breaks out against the obstructing agency. No, he first invents the most bizarre monster of all his gallery of monsters, namely, the death instinct; and then he splits off from it an outwardly directed part which he calls 'the instinct of aggression'.

This operation is described in the volume *Civilization and its Discontents* (London, 1930). The relevant passage is:

Since the ego-instincts were found to be libidinal as well, it seemed for a time inevitable that *libido* should become synonymous with instinctual energy in general, as C. G. Jung had previously advocated. Yet there still remained in me a kind of conviction, for which as yet there were no grounds, that the instincts could not all be of the same nature. I made the next step in *Beyond the Pleasure Principle* (1920), when the repetition-compulsion and the conservative character of instinctual life first struck me. On the basis of speculations concerning the origin of life and of biological parallels, I drew the conclusion that, beside the instinct preserving the organic substance and binding it into ever larger units, [the sex instinct] there must exist another in antithesis to this, which would seek to dissolve these units and reinstate their antecedent inorganic state; that is to say, a death instinct as well as Eros; the phenomena of life would then be explicable from the interplay of the two and their counteracting effect on each other. It was not easy, however, to demonstrate the working of this hypothetical death instinct. The manifestations of Eros were conspicuous and audible enough; one might assume that the death instinct worked silently within the organism towards its disintegration [a sort of inverted *vis medicatrix naturae*], but that, of course, was no proof. The idea that part of the instinct became directed towards the outer world and then showed itself as an instinct of aggression and destruction carried us a step further [1] (p. 96 et seq.).

---

[1] I find the mode of thinking of instinct revealed in this paragraph to be quite shocking; and I venture to think that at least ninety-nine biologists in a hundred would feel much as I do about it. One of my general complaints is that

Freud concludes his account of the death instinct by saying : 'I can no longer understand how we could have overlooked the universality of non-erotic aggression and destruction, and could have omitted to give it its due significance in our interpretation of life.' Which is just one of those things that I also could never understand. However, the main point is that, at long last, Freud, having achieved the instinct of external aggression, by splitting it off from the death instinct, now recognizes it as an independent functional unit. He affirms clearly : 'the tendency to aggression is an innate, independent, instinctual disposition in man'.[1]

Freud, without having made any serious effort to determine what are the instinctive endowments of the human species (and totally ignoring the comparative method which in this connexion is all important) flies off in long tortuous and highly speculative discussions of the origins of various hastily assumed instincts. The passage here cited is a favourable specimen. The whole of his *Group Psychology* a less favourable one. Is it to be wondered at that, as Freud plaintively says : 'The assumption of the existence of a death instinct or a destruction instinct has roused opposition even in analytical circles.' It is yet another proof that even the worm may turn, or at least wriggle, if you treat him too roughly.

[1] op. cit. p. 102. Freud himself wrote many years ago : 'No knowledge would have been so important for the establishment of a sound psychology as some approximate understanding of the common nature and possible differences of the instincts.' Then why not attack the problem directly ? Why make all advance in this direction a process of slow and painful stepwise correction of initial false assumptions by means of

FREUD REVOKES ON SADISM AND MASOCHISM

When will Freud make a similar declaration about fear ? It seems but too probable that before he shall have made this step the shadows will close upon him. Yet in the *New Lectures* he makes some progress in this direction.

Before turning to this topic, let us note that, in setting out this new doctrine of the death instinct, Freud revokes one of his most popular dogmas, namely, that sadism and masochism are manifestations of *libido*, of the sex instinct or instincts. In *Civilization and its Discontents*, he teaches that both sadism and masochism are manifestations of the newly invented death instinct.

> Sadism, long known to us as a component-instinct of sexuality, would represent a particularly strong admixture of the instinct of destruction into the love impulse ; while its counterpart, masochism, would be an alliance between sexuality and the destruction at work within the self (p. 98).

The view thus adopted by Freud, to the effect that sadistic and masochistic behaviour are expressions not of the sex instinct alone, but of that instinct working in co-operation with other instincts, is one which I have long urged. Where

wild speculations on the possible origin of instincts in the dark abyss of ages long past ? One might even add, in face of this profoundly difficult problem which deeply concerns every student of human nature—Why ignore utterly the views of the many psychologists and biologists who have struggled with it long and arduously throughout the last century and a half ?

I still differ from Freud is in my view of the nature of these adjuvant and modifying impulses. While Freud regards them as two opposite modes of working of the death instinct, I have long regarded them as the impulses of the two opposed but independent instincts of self-assertion and of submission, respectively ; instincts which we are compelled to postulate by a wealth of facts unrelated to sex behaviour.

Still, Freud's change of view here is a great step in the right direction, and therefore to be welcomed ; in spite of the fact that it so largely robs these allied topics, sadism and masochism, of their charm for amateur psychologists and Freudians alike.

FREUD'S VIEWS ON FEAR IN PROCESS OF CHANGE

We have seen that, after long delay, Freud has recognized that the destructive aggressive impulse springs from ' an innate, independent, instinctual disposition ', one quite distinct from the sex instinct. There are grounds at least equally strong for giving a similar status to the impulse of retreat or escape, the impulse at work in all experiences of fear, terror, panic, dread, apprehension, in all behaviour that is timid, cautious, fearful. The evidence afforded by animal behaviour is overwhelming. Everywhere (except in the few animals protected in other ways) the impulse to flee to cover is kept on a hair-trigger ;

and its workings in the animals and in man run strikingly parallel.

But Freud, for some inscrutable reason, began by declaring that fear is in some sense an expression of *libido*, that just as *libido* can be converted or transmuted into tenderness, or into sadistic or masochistic impulses, so also it can be transformed into fear. He now revokes on this doctrine and to that extent may be said to have advanced towards recognition of the independence of fear ; yet his present views on fear are obscure.

In the chapter of the *New Lectures* devoted to ' Anxiety and Instinctual Life ', Freud begins by reviewing his former teaching on this topic. The whole thing is so confused as to make a concise summary impossible. But roughly it amounts to this. There are two kinds of anxiety,[1] the objective and the neurotic

> the former being what seems to us an intelligible reaction to danger . . . and the latter altogether puzzling and, as it were, purposeless. We then asked ourselves two questions ; ' What are people afraid of when they have neurotic anxiety ? '

---

[1] It seems that the ambiguity of the German word *Angst* has had a pernicious influence in this matter. The word is generally translated as ' anxiety ' ; and this word, which properly denotes a mode of experience very different from fear (cp. my *Outline of Psychology*), is then treated as synonymous with the word ' fear ', masking this important distinction and perpetuating a confounding of two very different modes of reaction and experience. And it seems clear that the word *Angst* works in similar confusing fashion.

and 'How can one bring this kind of anxiety into line with objective anxiety felt towards an external danger?' . . . The most frequent cause of anxiety-neurosis is undischarged excitation. A libidinal excitation is aroused, but is not satisfied or used; in the place of this *libido* which has been diverted from its use, anxiety makes its appearance. I even thought it was justifiable to say that this unsatisfied *libido* is directly transformed into anxiety.

Further:

> It is to the process of repression that we attributed the appearance of anxiety in hysteria and other neuroses. . . . It is the idea that undergoes repression and may be distorted so as to become unrecognizable; its associated affect is always turned into anxiety, regardless of its nature, whether, that is to say, it is aggression or love.

Neurotic anxiety thus generated can however turn into objective anxiety. Hence he sums up his old view:

> As an affective condition, anxiety is the reproduction of an old danger—threatening event; anxiety serves the purposes of self-preservation as being the signal of the presence of a new danger; it arises from *libido* that has become unusable for some reason or other, including the process of repression.

That is to say, he had taught that all anxiety is transformed *libido*, regarding 'objective anxiety' as a special form of neurotic anxiety.

Now he turns the whole story upside down. After announcing that 'the ego is the only seat of anxiety and that only the ego can produce and feel anxiety', he goes on to say that certain investigations, to his astonishment, have shown him that: 'It is not repression that creates the anxiety, but the anxiety is there first and creates the repression!' Object anxiety becomes primary and neurotic anxiety a derived form, and fear of castration becomes the prototype of all fear. His old doctrine that anxiety or fear is *libido* repressed and transformed (or alternatively, that what the fearful person is afraid of is his own *libido*) has to be given up. 'We can, however, no longer venture to say that.'

But Freud, since he still does not recognize fear as rooted in 'an innate, independent, instinctual disposition in man', one of the most powerful of all the dynamic factors of human nature, is at a loss to account for the repression, and falls back upon the pleasure-principle. 'We have adopted the view that the pleasure-pain principle is brought into action in response to the danger-signal, and plays a part in repression'; and again, the ego 'sets the all-powerful pleasure-pain principle in motion by means of the danger-signal'.[1] Thus:

> Neurotic anxiety has, under our hands, turned into objective anxiety, into anxiety felt towards certain external danger-situations. . . . What is feared, the object of anxiety, is always the emergence of a traumatic factor, which cannot be dealt with in accordance with the norms of the pleasure-principle.

---

[1] It is significant that what he has hitherto called 'the pleasure-principle' here becomes the pleasure-pain principle'. This change was necessary since pleasure cannot with any plausibility be invoked as an inhibiting or repressing principle.

But he sees that this is not the final word, that he has given up his old doctrine without having found anything satisfactory to put in its place. 'Here', he says, 'everything is in a state of flux and change.'[1] And he hints at the next step: 'From the pleasure-principle to the instinct of self-preservation is a long way; and the two tendencies are far from coinciding from the first.' Yet it looks as though, given time, Freud will some day announce that he has travelled over this long way, and will exclaim: 'I can no longer understand how we could have overlooked the universality of non-erotic fear'; and will affirm that the tendency to escape from certain situations is an innate, independent, instinctual disposition in man, just as it so obviously is in all the higher species of animals.

FREUD'S MORE RECENT VIEWS ON THE TENDER IMPULSE

I regret that I find only slight parallel development in respect of another tendency of our nature, namely, the tendency to succour, cherish and protect. If my *Social Psychology* was not grossly in error in identifying this tendency with the impulse 'of an innate, independent, instinctual disposition' (an instinct the primary function of which is the cherishing of the infant) and in seeing in this impulse the sole root of truly altruistic activity

[1] *New Lectures*, p. 121.

of every kind, this remains one of the most urgent questions at issue between psycho-analysis and social psychology.[1] For Freud has always taught that this tender impulse is a manifestation of the sex-instinct, that it results from a transmutation of part of the *libido* consequent upon inhibition of its sensual aims. Psycho-analysis, he wrote in his *Group Psychology*,

> gives us courage to assert that whenever we come across a tender feeling it is the successor to a completely 'sensual' object-tie with the person in question or rather with that person's prototype (or *imago*).[2]

It will avail nothing to repeat here the arguments I have used before; to point to the unmistakable manifestations of this instinct in all the mammalian species and its functioning in

[1] Possibly we may see a first step in this direction in the following passage from *Civilization and its Discontents*: 'Individual development seems to us a product of the interplay of two trends, the striving for happiness, generally called "egoistic", and the impulse towards merging with others in the community, which we call "altruistic".'

[2] And that this view is still held is shown by the following passage from *New Lectures*: 'We have also grounds for the differentiation of what we call "*aim-inhibited*" instincts; these proceed from familiar sources and have unambiguous aims but come to a stop on their way to satisfaction, with the result that a permanent object-cathexis and an enduring driving force come into being. Of such a kind, for instance, is the feeling of affection, whose source undoubtedly lies in sexual needs but invariably renounces their gratification' (p. 146).

entire independence of the sex-instinct ; to adduce all the evidences that the sexual and the parental instincts vary independently of one another. I will therefore use two new arguments ; encouraged by Freud's tardy recognition of the independence of the aggressive instinct, to hope that, in this more important and more subtle problem of the tender impulse, he may yet come round to agreement with my view.

One of the very few psychologists to whose views Freud refers with respect is Arthur Schopenhauer. I will therefore invoke the aid of Schopenhauer in this matter. Schopenhauer is one of the very few psychologists of high rank who explicitly recognize in the constitution of man a specifically altruistic element or tendency. The working of this tendency, called by him 'loving kindness', is the theme of the most brilliant and by far the most convincing of all his writings, his essay on 'The Basis of Morals'. He argues convincingly that all truly moral conduct springs from, or is (in part at least) motivated by this tendency ; that all conduct in which this motive plays no part, no matter how objectively admirable, how comformable to all moral precepts it may be, is not truly moral. This is the most vital psychological question underlying all theory of morals. It was therefore a delight to me to find that, in the conclusion at which I had arrived in my *Social Psychology*, I had been anticipated by this great thinker.

Of course, Schopenhauer, his essay being pre-Darwinian, did not identify this altruistic factor in man's constitution with the parental instinct which man has in common with most of the higher animals. But there can be little doubt that, if he had written on this topic fifty years later than the date of his essay, he would have done so; preferring this biological generalization to the metaphysical assumption by which he 'explained' the altruistic impulse and, at the same time, ruined the chief virtue and beauty of his thesis, namely, the full recognition of truly altruistic motivation; the metaphysical assumption, namely, that we all are but fragments of one being and that, therefore, any man, when he succours another, is but doing good to himself.

The second new argument with which I appeal to Freud is the following. Freud accepts the Lamarckian principle of heredity and evolution, the 'transmission of acquired characters'.[1] Now Freud describes the tender impulse as becoming split off, or differentiated, from the sex instinct by the process of inhibition of the sexual aims of that instinct. And he assumes that this process

[1] I do not know that he has made any explicit avowal of such acceptance; but of late years his writings have implied such acceptance more and more clearly. In this he has followed the lead of Dr. C. G. Jung, who has from the first implicitly assumed the validity of the Lamarckian principle. I, on the other hand, have conducted throughout the last fifteen years a laborious experiment which brings every year a little more positive evidence in its support.

of individual development has been repeated in all normal men and women through countless generations of mankind. His *Totem and Taboo* and his *Group Psychology* are largely devoted to expounding this process of differentiation in successive generations of very primitive men. It would then be only consistent with other instances in which Freud assumes the evolution of new instinctual tendencies in Lamarckian fashion, to assume that this tender impulse must also have become an innate independent factor of the human species, since it is assumed to have been generated within and operative within successive generations through hundreds of thousands or millions of years. I cannot myself accept this view of the evolution of the tender impulse ; but I am content to postpone problems of evolution, until we shall have attained to some tolerable degree of agreement about the constitution of man as he at present exists.

LAST STAND OF THE *LIBIDO* THEORY

The third kind of development of Freud's doctrine of the instincts is illustrated by the derivation from the sex instinct of an innate predisposition to submit and obey, as described in his *Group Psychology* (cp. Appendix II).

THE TOTTERING DOCTRINE OF THE *LIBIDO*

It is clear that Freud's original assumption of two kinds of instincts, the one kind which inhibits and the other (the libidinous) which suffers inhibition, has led him into many difficulties and necessitated many sweeping changes in his account of the instincts ; changes which must raise in the most uncritical reader serious doubts as to the theory of the *libido*. At one time Freud seemed on the point of giving up that theory. He wrote :

> There is therefore a constant transformation of ego-*libido* into object-*libido*, and of object-*libido* into ego-*libido*. But, if this is so, the two cannot differ from each other in their nature, and there is no point in distinguishing the energy of the one from that of the other ; one can either drop the term *libido* altogether, or use it as meaning the same as psychic energy in general (*New Lectures*, p. 133).

But Freud saves himself from this threatening collapse of the *libido* theory by his invention of the death-instinct ; for this now provides the other form of psychic energy which, as the theory requires, may be set over against the *libido* as of a different nature. Thus he escapes for a time from the necessity of discarding all that is distinctive in his doctrine of the *libido* ; in this way he persuades himself that he may still hold fast to his perfectly groundless old assumption of two radically different kinds of instinctive energies, those liable to repression and those that effect repression of them.

Freud, then, still hangs on to his old dogma that in every case the protective tender impulse is a manifestation of aim-inhibited *libido*. And he has not yet revoked on curiosity as a form of sexual activity. He has not recognized disgust, nor yet self-assertion, as independent innate tendencies. Nevertheless it is clear that the once all-pervading sex-instinct is breaking up, is being replaced by an array of independent native tendencies, and that the doctrine of the all-efficient *libido* is therefore breaking down.

It is still true that, as Freud himself says: 'The theory of the instincts is, as it were, our mythology. The instincts are mythical beings, superb in their indefiniteness.' Yet they are becoming under his hands a little less superb, less mythical, and more definite.

RECENT CHANGES IN FREUD'S THEORY OF REPRESSION

Freud's theory of repression and the changes which have been rung on it by him, is a story closely bound up with his doctrine of the instincts and the *libido*. But it merits separate review. It is perhaps Freud's greatest service to have shown us the great role of repression and of the continuing subconscious activities of repressed tendencies. He has naturally been much concerned to evolve a theory of repression which shall reveal the nature of the repressing forces and the mode of their operation.

Freud's first rough answer to this question was to the effect that there must be instincts of two kinds, those which repress and those which suffer repression. His medical work had impressed him with the frequency of repression of sexual tendencies and with the power of repressed sexual inclinations to play havoc with the health and happiness of his patients. Therefore, he said, the sex impulses are those which are liable to repression. And, in looking round for the repressing forces, he seems to have argued as follows: The function of the sex-instinct is to secure the perpetuation of the species, a task which often involves the sacrifice of the individual. There must be an instinct (or instincts) whose function it is to preserve the individual, and this must be the natural opponent or antagonist of the sex-instinct. An instinct of self-preservation must, then, be the repressing agent; and this was at first identified with hunger and thirst. But it soon became clear that neither hunger nor thirst, nor both together, would suffice as the tendencies that enter into conflict with the libidinous tendencies, inhibit, repress, transform them, and direct them to ends quite other than reproduction.

For a time, especially the time when Freud was elaborating his theory of dreams, a mythical entity, the censor, was devised to do the work of keeping down and out of consciousness the quasi-personal libidinous tendencies. At this stage the question—What are the forces which induce repression? remained without any definite answer. Repression was ascribed vaguely to the influences of organized society, of training, of education, of punishment, ' the thick stick ' of the horde-father and of his surrogates or substitutes, the representatives of law and order in general. But how these influences worked, what energies or forces they evoked and brought to bear upon the libidinous tendencies was not made clear.

In the *Group Psychology* (cp. Appendix II) a special instinct to secure submission to the horde-father was evolved, as a special differentiation from the sex-instinct. And to this, which is the essential dynamic factor in all suggestion, a principle role in repression might well be assigned. Yet it was disqualified for this role by the fact that it was derived from the sex instinct and belonged, therefore, to the libidinous group of instincts whose nature it is to be repressed, rather than to repress.

Then, as Freud says : ' Our investigation of the neuroses led us to regard the ego as the restricting and repressing force ' (*New Lectures*, p. 125). And in order that the ego might have the dynamic quality implied by this role, it was invested with a group of ego-instincts. These have remained undefined, indeed shrouded in complete mystery, except that certain passages imply that hunger and thirst are of their number.[1]

Nevertheless, the ego and an outgrowth from it, the super-ego, became more prominent ; and

[1] e.g. ' This peculiarity [inflexibility] does not apply to all the ego-instincts but only to those of hunger and thirst ' (*New Lectures*, p. 127).

to them have been assigned of late years, mainly if not exclusively, the function of effecting repression ; and more lately still the function has been concentrated in the super-ego.

The super-ego, which becomes the special enforcer of moral precepts,[1] is formed from the ego by a process of transmutation of instincts (presumably of the always undefined ego-instincts) in which process ' identification ' with the parents plays a leading role—but what ' identification ' is remains obscure.[2]

Further still, the super-ego becomes ' the vehicle of the ego-ideals by which the ego measures itself, towards which it strives, and whose demands for ever-increasing perfection it is always

[1] ' The super-ego has the ego at its mercy and applies the most severe moral standards to it ; indeed it represents the whole demands of morality, and we see all at once that our moral sense of guilt is the expression of the tension between the ego and the super-ego ' (*New Lectures*, p. 83).

[2] ' I am myself not at all satisfied with this account of identification, but it will suffice if you will grant that the establishment of the super-ego can be described as a successful instance of identification with the parental function ' (*New Lectures*, p. 86).

I have little doubt that under the term ' identification ' Freud confuses two processes each of which is of great importance for the development of the individual, namely, firstly the growth of a sentiment of respect or of admiration for a particular person ; secondly, the extension to that person of the self-regarding sentiment. Both processes are described and discussed at more length in my *Social Psychology*.

striving to fulfil'. And: 'Now that we have posited a special function within the ego to represent the demand for restriction and rejection, i.e. the super-ego, we can say that repression is the work of the super-ego—either that it does its work on its own account or else that the ego does it in obedience to its orders' (*New Lectures*, p. 93).

Now it is clear that this account leaves a great gap; it leaves unanswered the fundamental question—How are accomplished the fundamental repressions which lead to the formation of the Oedipus complex in the infant? What forces effect those early repressions which result in all that Freud used to call 'the Unconscious'? For the super-ego, which is now said to be the great repressing agency (however obscure the nature of the 'transmuted' instincts which work in it) is itself described as a late product of individual development, and indeed as successor and heir to the vanishing Oedipus complex; the latter, therefore, cannot be the product of repression by the super-ego. And Freud himself has discovered another objection; namely, he has found reason to believe that the ego-instincts are themselves libidinal (cp. p. 77) and therefore (according to his fundamental assumption of two classes of instincts of radically different and opposed nature) must be among the repressed, rather than themselves repressors.

It seems to have been in view of these difficulties that Freud invented the death-instinct and substituted for his old original two classes of instincts which enter into conflict (the sex-instincts and the self-preservative or alternatively the ego-instincts) two new classes :

> We have to distinguish two classes of instincts, one of which, Eros, or the sexual instincts, is by far the more conspicuous and accessible to study. It comprises not merely the uninhibited sexual instinct proper and the impulses of a sublimated or aim-inhibited nature derived from it, *but also the self-preservative instinct which must be assigned to the ego*. . . . The second class of instincts was not so easy to define, in the end we came to recognize sadism as its representative.[1]

Here the self-preservative and the ego-instincts (which for half a lifetime have been dogmatically put forward as the great repressing forces) are lumped together with the sex-instincts as libidinal and therefore liable to repression. While the death-instinct (of which masochism is one expression and sadism and all outwardly aggressive and destructive behaviour are others) becomes the opposing force. And if one pertinaciously insists on trying to say what, in Freud's view at the

[1] *The Ego and the Id*, p. 55, italics mine. The same doctrine, the new pair of opposed forces, is repeated in the *New Lectures* : ' And now the instincts in which we believe separate themselves into two groups : the erotic instincts, which are always trying to collect living substances together into ever-larger unities, and the death-instincts which act against that tendency ' (p. 139).

present time, is the great agent of repression, perhaps the best guess one could make would be that it is the death-instinct or its sadistic component, which, when the super-ego takes shape, is incorporated in the latter as its principle if not sole energetic component. And this interpretation is borne out by the statement that the super-ego, which has been said to be the great repressing agency, ' makes the dangerous aggressive impulses its own ', and that the ego ' has to submit itself to the destructive impulses of aggression '.

The most probable view as to Freud's present doctrine regarding repression may, then I submit, be stated as follows : In the years of infancy and childhood repression is effected by the crude death-instinct or instinct of aggression. In later life this instinct becomes incorporated into the structure of the super-ego, which from this time on plays the role of repressing agent.

I, for one, should be glad to think that this is Freud's present teaching. For it represents a rough approximation to the view of the higher forms of control which I put forward in my *Social Psychology* (cp. p. 104).

FREUD'S ORIGINAL ASSUMPTION OF TWO KINDS OF INSTINCTS UNTENABLE

Yet this view still leaves on our hands a problem insoluble along the lines of Freud's fundamental assumption of two groups of instincts, the one group, the libidinous, which suffer inhibition and repression, and the other instinct, or group of instincts, which does the inhibiting and the repressing. For the aggressive instinct is, by Freud's own showing, liable to inhibition and repression.

It is by no means easy to satisfy the requirements of this civilization and to feel comfortable in its midst, because the restriction of the instincts which it involves lays a heavy psychological burden on our shoulders. Now what we have recognized as true of the sexual instincts holds to the same extent, and perhaps to an even greater extent, for the other instincts, for those of aggression. It is they above all that make communal existence difficult and threaten its permanence. The limitation of aggression is the first and perhaps the hardest sacrifice which society demands from each individual (*New Lectures*, p. 123).

There remains then still on our hands, or rather on Freud's, the old question—*Quis custodes custodiet?* What forces shall control and repress the great repressor, the instinct of aggression?

It is true that Freud follows the sentence last cited with the remark: 'We have learnt in what an ingenious way this unruly element is tamed'; referring here to the instinct of aggression. But if he has learnt this secret, he has not revealed it. I at least, after the most earnest search, can find in Freud's pages no indication of an answer to the problem.

I submit, with all respect to Freud, that his first hasty assumption of two opposed groups of instincts (one which suffers repression and the other which does all the repressing) is groundless error; that to cling obstinately to it amidst all changes, as Freud does,[1] is to raise perfectly gratuitously an insoluble pseudo-problem. I submit that the true answer to the problem of the repressing forces is that assumed in my *Outline of Abnormal Psychology*, namely, that any two instinctive tendencies may and do enter into conflict with one another, in so far as they work or strive towards incompatible goals; and that therefore every one may play a part in effecting repression of another; and that, as personality develops, the conflicts and co-operations of instinctive impulses are largely regulated by the systems into which they become organized (systems which I have described as the sentiments) and by the hierarchical system of the sentiments which is character.[2]

Some such scheme as I have sketched offers, I submit, the only solution of this very fundamental problem consistent with the hormic psychology, that theory of human nature which

[1] The reader will remember that he has promulgated in turn three distinct doctrines about the nature of the repressing instincts: first, they were the self-preservative instincts, identified with hunger and thirst; secondly, they were the undefined ego-instincts; thirdly, they were the aggressive or death instincts.

[2] At the more primitive levels, the fear-impulse playing the largest role as inhibitor and repressor, by reason of its great strength and of the fact that it is very apt to be opposed in tendency or direction to other impulses.

sees in the instinctive impulses the forces which activate all our mental life, sustain and regulate all our activities.

STILL OTHER DOCTRINES OF REPRESSION SUGGESTED BY FREUD

But Freud's psychology, though so largely hormic, is not purely hormic. The hormic theory is complicated by the assumption of the pleasure-pain principle and the reality principle, as dynamic mechanisms which operate alongside the instinctive impulses. And throughout Freud's pages are scattered remarks about these obscure ' principles ' or ' mechanisms ' which lead one to ask whether these are not after all, in his view, the great repressing agents.

At one stage of the discussion we are led to suppose that the ego exerts its control over, its inhibition and repression of, the libidinous impulses by bringing into play the mechanism of ' the reality-principle '. The ego, we are told,

> interpolates between desire and action the procrastinating factor of thought. . . . In this way it dethrones the pleasure-principle, which exerts undisputed sway over the processes of the *id*, and substitutes for it the reality-principle, which promises greater security and greater success (*New Lectures*, p. 101).

But here the same difficulty (if in less degree) arises as with the super-ego. The reality-principle, or its mechanism, is said to be a comparatively late product of individual development.

How then can it effect repression of the libidinous impulses of the infant?

Other passages suggest the possibility that the mechanism of the pleasure-pain principle is the fundamental repressing agent? And this raises the further question—Has the pleasure-pain principle one mechanism only, or two, a pleasure mechanism and a pain-mechanism? Some passages imply the latter view, as when we read: 'We interpret "pain" as implying a heightening and pleasure a lowering of energic cathexis.' For, if the effects are opposite, there are presumably two mechanisms. Yet perhaps it is one mechanism only, a pleasure-pain mechanism which works one way for pleasure, and for pain goes into reverse-gear. For this latter view seems to be implied when we are told that 'the *id*, guided by the pleasure-principle, that is, by the perception of "pain", guards itself against these tensions', tensions 'introduced by the claims of Eros'.

Lastly, the *New Lectures* contain yet another vaguely formulated doctrine of repression.

> It is not the repression that creates the anxiety [as he had formerly taught], but the *anxiety* is there first and *creates the repression*! But what sort of anxiety can it be? It can only be fear of a threatening external danger; that is to say, objective anxiety.

Now this is said only of repression of the boy's libidinous impulses towards his mother; and the fear here invoked as the repressing force is specifically fear of castration, fear evoked by the threats of the parent.[1]

Further :

> Fear of castration is naturally not the only motive for repression ; to start with, it has no place in the psychology of women ; they have, of course, a castration-complex, but they cannot have any fear of castration. In its place, for the other sex, is found fear of the loss of love (p. 113).

And both of these forms of fear are in some sense substitutes for the fear created by the experience of birth.

Here it almost looks as though Freud were admitting fear as an ' innate, independent, instinctual disposition in man ' and making of it the great agent of repression. But no ! For some obscure reason, as we have seen above, Freud,

[1] ' We have, however, not yet said what the real danger is that the child fears as a result of his being in love with his mother. It is the punishment of castration, the loss of his penis ' (p. 114). Apparently the doctrine is that the dutiful father in all ages has threatened his infant son with castration as a punishment for masturbation ; and for some inscrutable reason every infant has falsely interpreted this as a threat of punishment for libidinous approaches to his mother. For, since the infant's libidinous attachment to his mother was first revealed to the world by Freud, it is clear that in the pre-Freudian ages, fathers cannot have created the Oedipus complex by threatening castration for such libidinous approaches. And even in the present age, it can only be a relatively few highbrow fathers who make such threats. The common unenlightened father, being ignorant of Freud's theories, must still threaten castration for masturbation merely.

though he frequently comes very near to recognizing the fear impulse as a primary one, always draws back as follows :

> We have discovered two new facts . . . first, that anxiety causes repression, and not the other way round as we used to think, and secondly, frightening *instinctual* situations can in the last resort be traced back to *external* situations of danger. Our next question will be—How can we picture the process of repression carried out under the influence of anxiety ?

Freud's answer to this crucial question runs as follows :

> the ego anticipates the satisfaction of the questionable impulse, and enables it to reproduce the painful feelings which are attached to the beginning of the dreaded danger-situation. Thereupon the *automatic mechanism of the pleasure-pain principle* is brought into play and *carries through the repression* of the dangerous impulse (p. 118, italics mine).

And again, the ego ' by means of a danger-signal sets in motion the automatic pleasure-pain mechanism '.

After all, then, although repression is sometimes ' carried out under the influence of anxiety ', anxiety or fear is not the repressing force. It would seem that the fear serves merely to warn the ego of danger ; that thereupon the ego responds by putting up a danger-signal, which in turn ' sets in motion the automatic pleasure-pain mechanism ', which mechanism performs the act of repression. Presumably, therefore, this mechanism contains within itself the energy required for such repression.

Be it observed that this final word leaves us still quite in the dark as to how repression is effected. Freud merely postulates 'a mechanism' to do the trick, without offering the least suggestion as to the nature or mode of operation of that 'mechanism'. The question arises—is the word 'mechanism' thus used appreciably superior to the word 'faculty' as used by the most abandoned of faculty psychologists?

Further, be it noted, this latest volume sets forth at least two new and quite different, and therefore rival, theories of repression: first, the aggressive instinct as the universal repressor; secondly, anxiety as the repressor, working not by its own energy or force but by warning the ego to set in action its automatic pleasure-pain mechanism. Though whether the ego, when it responds, throws that mechanism into forward or reverse gear, is not made clear.

I venture to think it is not too optimistic to see in all this confused struggle of Freud against his self-imposed barrier (the assumption that the instincts must be of two kinds, the repressing and the repressed) progress towards the view I have taken, namely that the repressing function as exercised by one tendency on another is reciprocal. If indeed repression be (as seems most probable) a special form of inhibition; then this view is rendered almost inevitable. For it is clear that, in both men and animals, *the strongly excited impulse of the sex-instinct can and does inhibit other tendencies*.

THE PASSING OF THE OEDIPUS COMPLEX

I have already mentioned the fact that, as long as ten years ago, Freud had thrown to the growing limbo of his discarded errors the doctrine that the Oedipus complex is a constituent of 'the Unconscious' of men in general. I note now only that he stands by this great renunciation in his more recent publications. I find this clearly expressed in a number of passages.

The paper reprinted in this volume as Appendix IV [1] shows Freud's teaching in this matter up to the year (1925) in which it was written. Lest it be supposed that this revocation was merely a temporary aberration on his part, I refer the reader to two more recent works. In *The Ego and The Id* (1927) Freud writes of 'the dissolution of the Oedipus complex' as a normal incident of development in the young boy.

> Along with the dissolution of the Oedipus complex the object-cathexis of the mother must be given up. Its place may be filled by one of two things: either an identification with the mother or an intensified identification with the father. We are accustomed to regard the latter outcome as the more normal. . . . In this way the passing of the Oedipus complex would consolidate the masculinity in the boy's character.

---

[1] *The Oedipus Complex, an Attempt to estimate its Role and Importance.*

And in the volume, *New Introductory Lectures on Psycho-Analysis* (1933) Freud maintains no less explicitly the revised doctrine ; he writes, e.g. (p. 87) :

> When the Oedipus complex passes away the child must give up the intense object-cathexes which it has formed towards its parents . . . the super-ego does not attain to full strength and development if the overcoming of the Oedipus complex has not been completely successful. . . . At the time at which the Oedipus complex makes way for the super-ego. . . .

Again (p. 120) :

> In other instances *it seems to undergo complete destruction*, in which case its *libido* is finally diverted into other channels. I have suggested that *this is what happens where the Oedipus complex is dealt with normally*. In this desirable state of affairs, the Oedipus complex would thus not merely be repressed, but would be *actually destroyed* in the *id* (italics mine).

And again, since every male infant practises masturbation (at least in Vienna), and every parent threatens to castrate him as punishment for such conduct (again in Vienna) :

> the threat of castration forces him [the average normal boy] to give up this attitude. Under the influence of the danger of losing his penis, he abandons his Oedipus complex ; it is repressed and in the most normal cases entirely destroyed, while a severe super-ego is set up as its heir.

I point out in passing an inevitable implication of this reformed doctrine ; it becomes a moral obligation on every father to threaten to castrate his little son ; for only under the pressure of fear thus inspired will the boy consent to abandon his Oedipus complex. One is forcibly reminded of an equally famous parental prescription : ' Speak roughly to your little boy and whip him when he sneezes. He only does it to annoy because he knows it teazes.' A nice question arises : Does a threat to cut off the nose prevent a sneeze as effectively as a threat to cut off the penis induces abandonment of the Oedipus complex ?

But, seriously, can threats, even threats of castration, so easily destroy or even ' repress ' a complex ; especially that (allegedly) most deep-rooted, universal, earliest and most terrible of all complexes, the Oedipus ? And, more seriously still, I urge upon Freud and all Freudians, this question : The main, if not the sole, ground for the assumption that every infant acquires an Oedipus complex (or in the case of the female infant its equivalent) was the alleged fact (alleged by Freud and accepted by his followers as a main feature of his system) that this complex manifests itself in every adult (in dreams or otherwise). But Freud has now declared unequivocally that in the normal adult the Oedipus complex does not exist. What justification is there for continuing to insist that this complex is formed in every child ? If this doctrine were established by irrefutable and unquestionable evidence, we should have to accept and make the best of a horrible situation. But, when its main foundation is acknowledged by the founder himself to have been a mass of error, why continue to inflict on a civilization already chastened and distraught, a doctrine which is not only horrible to all natural persons, but also vastly destructive of family relations and domestic happiness ? [1]

[1] Since the testimony of Freud, Jung and Adler against the existence of the Oedipus complex in the general run of men has proved insufficient to shake the faith of the general run of Freudians, I will point out that the eminent anthropologist, Prof. E. Westermarck, has recently subjected the Oedipus complex doctrine to a searching examination and returns a verdict utterly adverse (*Three Essays on Sex and Marriage*, London, 1934). I will add also the testimony of a medical psychologist experienced in the practice of psychotherapy, Dr. W. H. Sheldon. In a volume shortly to be published (from which he kindly allows me to make citations) he writes: 'These parental sexual fixations of remembered childhood can be suggested readily enough to neurotic minds and can be teased up delightfully into the dimensions of a general alibi.' Again, ' So far as I am aware, a truly sexual fixation of a practically important nature between parent and child rarely if ever occurs except in low caste families living under conditions of bad domestic hygiene. It is common enough for unhealthful, unwise, or selfish, affectional and dominational relations to become established, especially between mothers and sons and between fathers and daughters. But these are not sexual problems, even by greatly stretching the meaning of that term.' Yet again, the same author writes : ' The psycho-analytic slang of Oedipus and castration complexes and overshadowing parental fixations has filtered into the common consciousness . . . through a certain borderline element in the medical profession who, except for their technical instruction in their profession are often incredibly immature and unimaginative persons.'

I know that to give up this dogma would require an immense effort on the part of all Freudians. It would be like forswearing one's totem animal. Nevertheless I call upon them in the name of humanity to make this great renunciation.

FREUD'S VIEW OF THE ROLE OF SUGGESTION IN THERAPY

The list of major changes in Freud's teaching may be closed by brief reference to one which intimately affects his therapeutic principles. Freud began his psycho-analytic work by using 'suggestion' in hypnosis as an aid to both exploration and re-adjustment. Then followed a long period during which he deprecated all use of suggestion; and his followers, including Dr. C. G. Jung, looked upon the use of hypnotic suggestion with almost pious horror. The 'transference' and the influence exerted by the physician on his patient during the time the 'transference' relation obtains was made the key-process in all psycho-therapy. I have long urged that what is called 'transference' is essentially the work of a specific instinct of submission, the evocation in the patient of the submissive impulse and attitude towards the physician.[1]

[1] I do, of course, not doubt that some women fall in love with their physicians. And I should suppose that when subjected to 'analysis' they are particularly liable to this troublesome result. It seems to me that the sex impulse whenever and however aroused is peculiarly apt to attach

I submit that Freud has come very near to the acceptance of that view. As we have seen, he now attributes all 'suggestion' (both waking and hypnotic) to a special innate instinctual disposition; and he recognizes that suggestion plays a large part in psycho-analytic treatment. As long ago as 1912, he wrote, in an article on *The Dynamics of the Transference*,[1] 'In so far we readily admit that the results of psycho-analysis rest upon a basis of suggestion.'

SUMMARY AND MORAL OF THE STORY

I must devote my few remaining minutes to an attempt to characterize this not yet completed story and to point its moral; the story of the rise of psycho-analysis and of its gradual transformation (by way of its excursions into the field of social problems) into a system of psychology acceptable to sober and scientific students of human nature.

Professor Freud set out as an eager student of the neuroses with such preparation only as a medical education affords, that is to say, without having made himself acquainted with what had been said and thought on the problems of human nature by a long series of the most powerful in-

itself to any member of the opposite sex (or even of the same) who may happen to be within range and to be in the least degree presentable. Is not this the key to the great art of seduction as practised by both sexes?

[1] *In Collected Papers.*

tellects the human race has yet produced ; and, further, he was unhampered by any too scrupulous respect for the mechanical prejudices of the nineteenth century, which at that time were enjoying their greatest vogue and triumph.

With great perspicacity and originality, he put his finger on the most fundamental factor of neurotic disorder, the conflict of competing tendencies. Forthwith he concentrated his attention on the commonest form of such conflict, the form in which the sex tendency is one of the principle parties to the conflict. While still his attention was confined to the neuroses and allied phenomena, especially dreams, he made an array of highly general fundamental assumptions about the constitution and working of human nature.

Not delaying to check and correct these hastily formed assumptions by any comparative survey of human and animal varieties of nature and function, he began to apply them, together with ways of thinking determined by them, to the problems of social life, especially those of primitive societies ; a sphere in which our total lack of sure knowledge of facts gave free play to his speculative fancy. Thus he complicated and added to his stock of assumptions, continuing to develop his scheme of human nature along the lines first adopted for the elucidation of the neuroses.

The first serious check came with the multitude of neurotic troubles produced by the battlefields of the Great War and also by the many severe back-of-the-front conflicts of the same period. For few of these lent themselves to interpretation strictly in terms of the assumptions hitherto chiefly relied upon by Freud ; and very many of these cases of war-neurosis were adequately interpreted and successfully treated in terms of much simpler assumptions.

A second serious check came from the field-anthropologists. For, though truly primitive man no longer exists, there still are communities of relatively primitive men ; and these afford a testing field for some of Freud's speculations about primitive man and society. And *on the whole the result of such testing has been adverse.* I refer here especially to Professors Westermarck, Seligman and Malinowski (all of this university, the latter two of whom approached this work strongly predisposed in favour of Freud's theories). As Professor Westermarck says, in concluding his long adverse essay on the Oedipus complex :

> Objections raised by the latter [i.e. sociologists and anthropologists] cannot be ignored by those whose faith in Freud as a psycho-analyst has made them ready to swallow the unfounded sociological presumptions of his theory.[1]

Recognizing the insufficiency of his system, Freud's vigorous and fertile mind pushed on with the task of improving it, and especially with the task of rendering it adequate to deal with social problems of many kinds. The changes intro-

[1] *Three Essays on Sex and Marriage*, London, 1934.

duced by him took three forms. First, he introduced further complications designed to patch up the weak spots of his system. Of this patch-work his later attempts to adapt his doctrine of child-development to the girl provide copious illustration; for, in his account of child-development as originally evolved, the boy alone had been kept in view. Many changes and additions were required: all the complicated story of penis-envy and so forth was added; still leaving the story, as Freud himself says, 'admittedly incomplete and fragmentary',[1] and, as I will venture to add, fantastic and improbable in an extreme degree.[2]

[1] *New Lectures*, p. 173.

[2] We are asked to believe, first, that every little girl invents for herself the fiction that her mother has deprived her of her penis; secondly, that the resentment and fear occasioned by belief in this fiction suffice to destroy her libidinous attachment to her mother, and to convert it into hatred for her. But, even if we could believe all this part of the story, a great difficulty remains unnoticed by Freud. The girl is said to form a libidinous attachment to her mother, just as the boy is said to do; and this attachment is so definitely sexual as to involve a clearly expressed 'desire to get the mother with child, as well as the corresponding one to have a child by the mother'. Now this pre-oedipal attachment of the girl to her mother, which we are told may last beyond the fourth year is distinctly asserted to be a *tender* attachment. And the *libido* is (by fundamental dogma) convertible into tenderness only by way of suppression or inhibition of its sexual aims. In the case of the boy the story is coherent; the father brings about the tender attachment of the boy to himself by his threats and beatings; which inhibit the sexual aims of the boy's sexual impulse directed to the mother and convert

These complicating supplementary hypotheses are, I venture to think, of minor importance. There is little room for doubt that most of them will be allowed to lapse and sink into oblivion, (like the Censor, the primal horde-father, and the universal Oedipus complex and other figures that once played leading roles).

Secondly, there are the great changes which have consisted in modifying with many twists and turns and finally in throwing overboard more or less completely a number of the assumptions, the too hasty and too sweeping generalizations, with which he had set out. Some of the chief of these

it, in part, into tender attachment to himself. But what inhibiting process converts the girl's *libido* directed to the mother into tenderness towards her? Are we to believe that (in Vienna) all mothers regularly beat their little daughters? That seems to be the plain implication. This astonishing chapter on 'The Psychology of Women' contains, besides a wealth of very tough and indigestible morsels of the kind just now indicated, a strangely naïve admission, namely, Freud remarks that during the early period of his work (when he held the sexual-trauma theory of the origin of neuroses): 'Almost all my female patients told me that they had been seduced by their fathers.' At a later time when Freud had given up the sexual-trauma theory, and had adopted the theory of the pre-Oedipal sexual fixation of the girl on her mother, the seduction phantasy still crops up as before; but now 'the seducer is invariably the mother' (*New Lectures*, p. 155). Could there be clearer evidence that what the Freudian analysts extract from their patients they first implant in them? Since their theories determine what they implant, is it not very natural that what they extract fits well with their theories?

I have briefly pointed to in these few lectures. And these discardings are the greatest of the advances.

The changes of a third kind consist in the discovery or invention of instincts previously ignored, but now serving to fill the gaps created by the changes of the second kind. Of these the instinct of aggression is the leading example.

MAJOR AGREEMENTS BETWEEN PSYCHO-ANALYSIS AND SOCIAL PSYCHOLOGY

Freud's psycho-analysis thus advances mainly by going backwards: Freud himself, aided in some degree by the less completely docile of his disciples, goes back upon his too hasty assumptions, one after another; painfully discovers the untenable nature of each in turn; and eventually, with a reluctant gasp, repudiates the error. If and when about as many more major errors shall have been jettisoned as have already been thus dealt with (especially the reality-principle, the pleasure-principle, the *libido* theory with its two radically different kinds of energy, the death-instinct, the over-emphasis on sex, strict determinism) and when some four or five further additions shall have been made to his list of major 'innate, independent, instinctual dispositions in man', then the Freudian system will be a strongly based and widely applicable social psychology. It will in many respects bear a strikingly close resemblance to the *Social Psychology* which I set forth in 1908; but it will embody a much richer and deeper appreciation of the range of subconscious activities, of the wide and subtle influences of conflict, of repression, of sublimation, of symbolism, of the genesis of symptoms, errors, myths and dreams.

OTHER POINTS OF AGREEMENT

In addition to the large and increasing number of major points of agreement between these two systems of social psychology which have been already indicated, it is, perhaps, worth while to point to certain other agreements which may not be very obvious.

The replacement of 'the Unconscious' by the *id* removes one leading difference. Further, Freud's four 'realms, regions or provinces into which we divide the mental apparatus of the individual', namely, the *id*, the ego, the super-ego and the ego-ideal (of which the second develops out of the first, and the third out of the second, and the fourth within the third) correspond to the four levels of function of my scheme: namely, (1) the purely instinctive level; (2) the level of control of the instinctive impulses which comes with increased range of foresight and the growth of self-consciousness and the concrete sentiments; (3) the level of self-conscious control and restraint of impulse that comes with the growth of the sentiment of self-regard or self-respect; (4) the topmost level which is achieved by the formation of the moral sentiments and an ideal of self shaped by the moral tradition. Freud's 'ego' is, in short, what in my *Social Psychology* is called character; while his super-ego (with its ego-ideal contained within it) corresponds to what in my book was called 'moral character'.

> The super-ego of the child is not really built up on the model of the parents, but on that of the parents' super-ego; it takes over the same content, it becomes the vehicle of tradition and of all the age-long values which have been handed down in this way from generation to generation . . . the ideologies of the super-ego perpetuate the past, the traditions of the race and the people.

These and a few other passages from the *New Lectures* show clearly that Freud is here, tardily and scantily, recognizing that highest level of functioning and the development of it under the influence of parents and other elders who embody the moral tradition. There is here no substantial difference between us; except that Freud merely points to the essential facts, while I have tried to supply in some detail, by aid of my theory of the sentiments, an account of the development, constitution and working of this highest stratum of the personality.[1]

[1] First in my *Social Psychology* as well as in various later books. If any one familiar with my *Social Psychology* reads pp. 90 and 91 of the *New Lectures*, he cannot fail to recognize in this one paragraph a kind of condensed and cryptic repetition of the main themes of my *Social Psychology* of 1908. I am not here accusing Freud of having read my *Social*

The passage cited in the footnote recognizes also a fact pointed out in my *Social Psychology* and insisted upon as the most fundamental fact and the most crucial problem for all moral psychology;

Psychology; I feel sure he has not. I am rejoicing in the fact that he is slowly arriving at identical views concerning the most crucial problems of *Social Psychology*. It seems worth while to cite this paragraph in full: 'But let us get back to the Super-ego. We have allocated to it the activities of self-observation, conscience and the holding up of ideals. It follows from our account of its origin that it is based upon an overwhelmingly important biological fact no less than upon a momentous psychological fact, namely, the lengthy dependence of the human child on its parents and the Oedipus complex; these two facts, moreover, are closely bound up with each other. For us the super-ego is the representative of all moral restrictions, the advocate of the impulse towards perfection, in short it is as much as we have been able to apprehend psychologically of what people call the "higher" things in human life. Since it itself can be traced back to the influence of the parents, teachers and so on, we shall learn more of its significance if we turn our attention to these sources. In general, parents and similar authorities follow the dictate of their own super-egos in the upbringing of children. Whatever terms their ego may be on with their super-egos, in the education of the child they are severe and exacting. They have forgotten the difficulties of their own childhood, and are glad to be able to identify themselves fully at last with their own parents, who in their day subjected them to such severe restraints. The result is that the super-ego of the child is not really built up on the model of the parents, but on that of the parents' super-ego; it takes over the same content, it becomes the vehicle of tradition, and of all the age-long values which have been handed down in this way from generation to generation. You may easily guess the fact, namely, that the moral sentiments (i.e. sentiments of love and hate for qualities of conduct and of character) of the child inevitably grow after the pattern of those which the parents and other admired and respected persons have acquired ; and thus become the embodiment and transmitters of the all-important moral tradition (the moral sentiments being the grounds of all moral valuations).

Freud has offered an explanation of this process of moulding in his theory of identification ; though I for one fail to find in this word ' identification ' more than a technical designation of the process ; and, as we have seen, Freud admits that he himself is ' not at all satisfied with this [his own] account of identification '. And indeed the theory amounts merely to the recognition of the

what great help is afforded by the recognition of the super-ego in understanding the social behaviour of man, in grasping the problem of delinquency, for example, and perhaps, too, in providing us with some practical hints upon education. It is probable that the so-called materialistic conceptions of history err in that they underestimate this factor. They brush it aside with the remark that the " ideologies " of mankind are nothing more than resultants of their economic situation at any given moment or superstructure built upon it. That is the truth, but very probably it is not the whole truth. Mankind never lives completely in the present ; the ideologies of the super-ego perpetuate the past, the traditions of the race and the people, which yields but slowly to the influence of the present and to new developments, and, so long as it works through the super-ego, plays an important part in man's life, quite independently of economic conditions.'

fact that ' when a boy identifies himself with his father, he wants to *be like* his father . . . his ego is altered on the model of his father ' (*New Lectures*, p. 86). My *Social Psychology* also offers an explanation of the process, namely, in terms of the sentiments of respect and admiration and of the principle of primitive passive sympathy.

But Freud still knows nothing of these things, nothing of such primitive sympathy, and nothing of the sentiments, which, at these higher levels of mental life, are the all-important dynamic factors. The facts of the simple sentiments for persons and concrete objects he describes in terms of object-cathexes ; but the later-developed more subtle sentiments, the sentiment of self-regard and the sentiments for abstract objects, he recognizes only by a few vague remarks about ' transmutation ' of instincts in the super-ego. It is true that he writes that the super-ego is ' the vehicle of the ego-ideal ' and that ' this ego-ideal is a precipitation of the old idea of the parents, an expression of the admiration which the child felt for the perfection which it at that time ascribed to them '. But in Freud's scheme the sentiment of admiration (like the sentiment of respect) has no place ; and though he is right in recognizing the role of admiration in the development of the highest stratum of personality, he cannot validly invoke its dynamic aid, so long as it remains, as it does in his scheme, a mere word.

THE OTHER SCHOOLS OF PSYCHO-ANALYSIS

I have perhaps sufficiently indicated my opinion of Dr. Alfred Adler's psychology, which, much to Freud's just annoyance, is commonly referred to as one of the schools of psycho-analysis. I will add only this concise estimate. It has a few great virtues and very many grave defects. Its value lies chiefly in the fact that it serves to show the large lay public which interests itself in psycho-analysis, that not all psycho-therapists agree with Freud—although most of that public seem incapable of recognizing the fact that there are hardly two points common to the doctrines of Freud and Adler.

As regards the considerable number of medical men who declare themselves disciples of Adler's *Individual Psychology*, I venture to think that their adherence may in many cases be accounted for as follows. Beginning to realize that medical psychology and psycho-therapeutics are fashionable and, perhaps, professionally important topics, the medical man, brought up in his medical school with scarcely a reminder, however slight, that there is a mental aspect to the human organism, turns to the Freudian literature. Finding after a time that he can make neither head nor tail of it; or that he cannot swallow much of it, or that, having swallowed it, he cannot stomach it, he turns away discouraged. And then when, like a young man deceived by finding his first love a cocotte, he looks around again, he is caught on the rebound by Adler's mellifluous and impeccable tones; craving release from torturing uncertainties and revolting paradoxes, longing for repose upon some simple and pure bosom, he sinks with a sigh of relief into the local *Society for Individual Psychology*, where he will hear nothing that will shock his sensibilities and nothing which will over-strain his cortical apparatus.

DR. C. G. JUNG'S PSYCHOLOGY

The third system of psychology generally classed as psycho-analytical is that of Dr. C. G. Jung. I may comment upon it only very briefly in the present connexion.[1]

The differences of the therapeutic methods taught by Freud and Jung, I am not here concerned to estimate. Two of Jung's contributions have interested me deeply. His distinction between introversion and extroversion has seemed to me important, though greatly in need of simplified definition in such terms as I have endeavoured to supply. But Jung's later attempts to establish eight (or is it sixteen?) important types of personality on this basis seems to me to have failed.[2]

[1] For my appreciation of it, as for other criticisms of Freud's teaching, cp. my *Outline of Abnormal Psychology*.

[2] Chiefly because it is based on the assumption of four distinct faculties (in the old sense of the word), namely, sensation, intuition, reason and feeling. But also because Jung persists in perpetuating one of the fundamental errors, now recently revoked by Freud, namely, the wide separation of the Unconscious from the conscious part of the mind.

But his main contribution to psychology has been his doctrine of the archetypal modes of thinking. This, if true, is profoundly important for Social Psychology. It is clear that this hypothesis must stand or fall with the Lamarckian principle of 'inheritance of acquired characters'; a truth in which Jung does not seem to have been interested.

Since I have always suspected that (in spite of Weissmann and all the Neo-Darwinians) the Lamarckian principle may be valid, I have been from the first open-minded towards and intrigued by Jung's doctrine of the Archetypes. When in 1919 and 1920 Dr. Jung was so kind as to investigate my dreams, he seemed to discover in them some faint traces of support for this doctrine. Since that date I have heard rumours to the effect that Dr. Jung, in the intervals between curing various millionaire American neurotics, was making expeditions to study the dreams of various primitive peoples; and these have stimulated me to look hopefully in Jung's later publications for further evidence in support of his interesting speculation—but in vain.

Every year that passes, without bringing from Jung, or from one or other of his disciples, new evidences of this kind, is a heavy blow against the doctrine of the archetypes; for, if that doctrine be true, comparative study of the dreams of groups of men of widely different racial origins should quickly bring a flood of evidence in its support. Hence, although my own experiment on the Lamarckian question has brought me year by year increasingly positive results,[1] my anticipation of the establishment of the archetypes has grown fainter and fainter.

Meanwhile Jung has withdrawn himself more and more completely from contact and discussion with common mortals like myself. And the pronouncements which reach this world from the cloud-capped Olympus on which he dwells may have been well calculated to sustain his old converts in the faith, but hardly of a nature to bring any new ones into the fold.[2]

[1] Cp. three reports in *British Journal of Psychology*, the last in vol. XIV, 1933.

[2] I cite what is presumably the latest of these, and highly characteristic, from Jung's introduction to *The Secret Ways of the Mind* (by G. W. M. Kranefeldt, London, 1934), 'My function as an investigator in the field of psychology consists chiefly in this . . . to break rudely in upon the situation, which is simple to the point of monotony from both of the other standpoints [those of Freud and of Adler] and to call attention to the inconceivable complexity of the soul as it really is. . . . If the human psyche is anything, it is inconceivably complicated and of an unlimited multiplicity; so that it cannot possibly be approached through a mere instinct psychology. I can only stop to gaze with admiration and awe at the depths and heights natural to the soul, whose non-spatial world conceals an untold abundance of images amassed and organically consolidated throughout millions of years of development. My consciousness is like an eye that penetrates into the most distant spaces, but it is the psychical non-ego which fills these spaces, though not spatially. And

A FINAL WORD

Now finally let me try to define two fundamental virtues which, as I said at the outset, are possessed by all the psycho-analytical schools and which are evidenced by the common applicability of their doctrines to problems of social life.

The first and most fundamental virtue common to all these schools is that they deal with human nature and human activities in terms which recognize that, from first to last and at every point in every aspect, they are teleological; not in any theological sense, but in the sense that all human activity is purposive, is a striving towards goals. It is not clear to me that Freud himself is aware of this fundamental virtue of his system; yet it is there in all his treatment, though somewhat obscurely expressed and in some degree hidden by his frequent postulation of what he calls 'mechanisms' and by his quite gratuitous insistence on rigid determinism.

In the work of Jung this virtue stands out more clearly and consciously. And the still more explicit adoption without reserve of a thoroughly purposive view of all human action by Adler is,

these images are not pale shadows, but powerfully active conditions of the psyche. The most that we may be able to do is to misunderstand them, but we can never rob them of their power by denying them.' I add that the author of this book succeeds in presenting the whole of Adler's psychology on ten small pages.

I venture to think, the virtue to which his teaching owes its success ; perhaps even more than to that extreme simplicity which renders it so eminently suited to simple minds.

For, when the psycho-analytic schools began to compete for attention with the various academic psychologies, the latter were for the most part still dominated more or less by the mechanistic prejudices of nineteenth-century science, as many of them still are, especially in America ; and they were in consequence rendered in many respects sterile and, especially, rendered inapplicable to the problems of social life. Hence the teachings of the Psycho-Analytic schools shone brightly by contrast. Hence they found in the field of Social Psychology a great province which the predominant mechanical psychologies had been, from their very nature, unable to occupy.

A second common virtue is the recognition and use by all these schools of the hormic principle, the principle that human activities are prompted and sustained by impulses and desires which spring from deeply-rooted innate dispositions (variously called propensities, instinctual dispositions or instincts).

As with the former virtue, Freud's psychology can claim this virtue only partially ; because he complicates his hormic psychology with the ' pleasure-pain principle ' and the utterly vague ' reality-principle ', both of which are treated as fundamental dynamic factors.

Both Jung and Adler in diverging from Freud without, so far as I know their writings, explicitly repudiating the hedonic principle (long discredited by all more discerning psychologists as a fundamental principle of action) have allowed both it and the ‘ reality-principle ’ to fall into the background and slide quietly out of the picture. They thus may claim for their systems, the virtue of full acceptance of the hormic principle.

APPENDIX I

AN EXAMINATION OF FREUD'S *TOTEM AND TABOO*: RESEMBLANCES BETWEEN THE PSYCHIC LIVES OF SAVAGES AND NEUROTICS [1]

PROFESSOR FREUD has turned his astonishingly fertile and ingenious mind to a new problem. Dr. Rivers has pointed out some years ago points of affinity between dreams and the myths of primitive peoples. Now Professor Freud comes forward with a far more ambitious scheme of application of his peculiar psychological principles. Briefly and baldly the aim of the book is to show that all totemism and taboo and, in consequence, 'the beginnings of religion, ethics, society and art meet in the Oedipus complex' (p. 260); that is to say, that all these things are rooted in the male infant's incestuous desire for his mother. The affirmation of the universality of such incestuous desire has become the foundation-stone of all Freudian psychology. Freud writes: 'We have gone so far as to declare that the relation to the parents instigated by incestuous longings is the central complex of the neurosis' (p. 29); and 'In every individual of the race the desire for it (i.e., incestuous union with the parent of the opposite sex) is unconscious, just as in the neurotic' (p. 53).

This is not the place for an examination of this fundamental dogma. We must rather accept it for the purpose of the argument, and must try to see how far its

[1] Reprinted from *Mind*, 1920.

acceptance enables Freud to throw new light on the problems of totem and taboo. For, if it should appear that he succeeds in this self-chosen task, the fact will lend support to this most disputable doctrine of the universal Oedipus complex.

The conclusions at which Freud arrives may be stated concisely and, I think, fairly, as follows. Totemism is the fundamental form of taboo from which all others are derived. The totem animal is essentially a substitute for the father. The prohibition of all intercourse with women of the totem clan is an extension of the prohibition against incest with the mother and is the root of all exogamy. ' The divinity that doth hedge a king ', the taboo of kings and chiefs, is due to the king's occupying the place of the father, to his exercising paternal authority and omnipotence, and the consequent transference to him of the man's normal attitude of jealous hatred towards his father. The taboo of the dead is a further and less direct extension of the same attitude; and all other forms of taboo are extensions of this attitude towards the dead, in so far as spirits or demons, analogous to the spirits of the dead, are conceived by the savage as surrounding and influencing him at all times and places. Gods were developed from totem animals by a further extension of the same attitude, as the notion of spiritual powers developed. ' The totem may have been the first form of the father substitute and the god a later one in which the father regained his human form ' (p. 245). Thus the observance of taboo is the beginning of ' conscience ' and morality; the rites of the dead are the beginnings of religion; and the exogamic relations of the totem clan are the beginnings of society.

Such in briefest outline are Freud's conclusions. The argument by which he seeks to establish them is twofold.

The one part consists in showing the resemblances between the attitude of the savage to his totem and other taboo objects and that of the neurotic, and in a less degree of the normal man, towards his father. The other part consists in showing how, these attitudes being postulated, savage societies may be supposed to have developed their particular forms of taboo and ritual. Let us consider first the former part.

The attitude of every man towards his father is 'ambivalent'. He hates him and desires to murder him, because his father enjoys sexual intercourse with his mother, on whom his own sexual *libido* is fixed. All this sexual jealousy is normally driven into 'the Unconscious' by the social prohibitions and the tenderness for the fatherly protector which naturally arises in response to the father's loving care. In the normal civilized man this repression is successful and continued; but in the neurotic and the savage (for all savages are more or less neurotic or at least in a condition very similar in many respects to neurosis) this repression is less complete, and the incompletely repressed hatred of the father works powerfully within him, alongside his desire for incest with his mother, determining many of his emotional attitudes and actions.

This 'ambivalence' of the emotional attitude towards the father is the key which Freud uses to unlock all doors in this obscure region. It is on showing a similar 'ambivalence' of attitude towards the totem, towards kings, towards the dead, and towards taboo objects in general that he chiefly relies for the justification of his scheme.

The second part of the argument consists in adopting Robertson Smith's view of the totem feast and the attractive hypothesis of the nature of primeval society which Atkinson and Andrew Lang erected on the basis of a suggestion of Charles Darwin. The combination of these two hypotheses with the principle of the great strength in savages of the 'ambivalent' attitude to the father, based on the incestuous desire of the mother, yields the following sketch of primitive society. The father or patriarch expels from the family circle his adolescent sons, in order that they may not share his rights over the females of the group. When the band of exiled brothers feels itself strong enough, they return, kill the father and eat him; then, being filled with remorse for the treatment of their tenderly (consciously) loved father (treatment to which they have been impelled by their unconscious jealousy of him), instead of satisfying their incestuous desires, they set up a strong barrier against such indulgence, in the form of the exogamic law or taboo against intercourse with the mother; and, since the father was a polygamist, or rather indulged himself indiscriminately with all females of the group, this taboo against incest affects all women of the group (they being regarded collectively and individually as mothers of all sons of the group). The father whom they have slain and eaten then becomes the totem; and the women of his group belong to his totem; and the horror of incest with them remains strong, just because the desire for the mother extends itself to all these wives of the father; for they are collectively the mothers of the revolting brothers, and a mother is by definition a woman with whom they unconsciously desire sexual intercourse. In the totem feast the brothers (i.e., the men of the totem clan) repeat ceremonially the slaying and devouring of the beloved father, thus giving vent once more to their unconscious hatred and, at the same time, renewing their sense of remorse and guilt, which is the foundation of all conscience and religion.

The taboo of kings and gods at a later stage of social evolution is a natural extension to these wielders of paternal authority of the ambivalent attitude of tender affection and of guilty remorse. And to the dead in general the same attitude becomes extended, because all death is regarded by savages as due to murder; and the sense of guilt of the patricides is so strong and the ambivalence of their emotional life is so habitual, that they feel themselves to be the murderers of all their relatives who die; and the more they love them, the more strongly do they unconsciously hate them, and therefore the more distinctly do they feel the sense of guilt and the fear of their shades.

It is advisable to substantiate this condensed account by citing a few of the most relevant passages.

> Psycho-analysis has revealed to us that the totem animal is really a substitute for the father, and this usually explains the contradiction that it is usually forbidden to kill the totem animal, that the killing of it results in a holiday and that the animal is killed and yet mourned [1] (p. 234).
>
> The expelled brothers joined forces, slew and ate the father, and thus put an end to the father horde. . . . Of course these cannibalistic savages ate their victim. This violent primal father had surely been the envied and feared model for each of the brothers. Now they accomplished their identification with him by devouring him and each acquired a part of his strength. The totem feast, which is perhaps mankind's first celebration, would be the repetition and commemoration of this memorable, criminal act with which so many things began, social organization, moral restrictions and religion (p. 236).

---

[1] Let not the innocent reader be misled into supposing that the psycho-therapeutic practice of Freud or of any of his followers is largely among male members of totem clans.

They hated the father who stood so powerfully in the way of their sexual demands and their desire for power, but they also loved and admired him. After they had satisfied their hate by his removal and had carried out their wish for identification with him, the suppressed tender impulses had to assert themselves. This took place in the form of remorse (p. 237).

This remorse forbade the killing of the totem except ceremonially.

They undid their deed by declaring that the killing of the father substitute, the totem, was not allowed, and renounced the fruits of their deed by denying themselves the liberated women. Thus they created the two fundamental taboos of totemism out of the sense of guilt of the son, and for this very reason this had to correspond with the two repressed wishes of the Oedipus complex (p. 238).

At first the brother clan had taken the place of the father horde and was guaranteed by the blood bond. Society is now based on complicity in the common crime, religion on the sense of guilt and the consequent remorse, while morality is based partly on the necessities of society and partly on the expiation which this sense of guilt demands.

This comprehensive scheme of explanation of all things in terms of 'the Oedipus complex' might be criticized by questioning the truth of its three basal hypotheses, namely, the universality of the Oedipus complex, Robertson Smith's view of the totem feast, and the Lang-Atkinson view of the nature of the primitive human group and the 'primal law'. It might also be criticized by pointing to things that it does not explain, totems which are not animals (such things as the sun, stars, rain, wind) and such taboos as those connected with agricultural operations or whatever other things and actions are of great economic importance to the savage. But Professor Freud's ingenuity would no doubt be equal to the task of extending his system of explanation to such things, also to tracing all of them back to the Oedipus complex. It is more profitable therefore to waive such objections, to grant to Freud his three basal hypotheses, and to inquire whether, these being given, the scheme as applied entails any insuperable difficulties.

One serious difficulty is lightly touched on by Freud himself.

> We know nothing about the origin of this ambivalence (the coincidence of love and hate towards the same object). It may be assumed to be a fundamental phenomenon of our emotional life. But the other possibility seems to me also to be worthy of consideration: that ambivalence, originally foreign to our emotional life, was acquired by mankind from the father complex, where psycho-analytic investigation of the individual to-day still reveals the strongest expression of it (p. 261).
>
> It can hardly have escaped anyone that we base everything upon the assumption of a psyche of the mass in which psychic processes occur as in the psychic life of the individual. Moreover, we let the sense of guilt for a deed survive for thousands of years, remaining effective in generations which could not have known anything of this deed. We follow an emotional process such as might have arisen among generations of sons that had been ill-treated by their fathers, to continue to new generations which had escaped such treatment by the removal of the father.

Freud here raises the question which is raised also in an acute form (but not, so far as I know, previously mentioned by him), by his doctrine of fixed universal symbols; the question namely of the validity of postulating well-formed racial innate ideas and racial sentiments or complexes. Jung has boldly recognized this problem and accepted such innate ideas, in his doctrine of universal ‘ archetypes ’ of thought ; and it is interesting to see that Freud is becoming alive to the same implication of his doctrines.

In the present state of biological opinion, the necessity of assuming such innate factors of the mind is an objection to the whole Freudian system ; but not a fatal one, for the possibility of the transmission of acquisitions by use-inheritance cannot be absolutely ruled out. But, if we grant such implanting in the racial mind of such ideas and tendencies by use-inheritance, we cannot allow Freud to play fast and loose with the principle, as he inclines to do. For he tells us that Westermarck is wrong in supposing the horror of incest to be innate—

> the experiences of psycho-analysis make the assumption of such an innate aversion to incestuous relations altogether impossible. They have taught, on the contrary, that the first sexual impulses of the young are regularly of an incestuous nature (p. 206).

It would be difficult indeed to admit that each of us inherits both a tendency to incestuous love and a horror of it ; and to admit this would be gravely disturbing to the whole Freudian system. We have, then, this curious situation. Freud asks us to admit that the remorse and sense of guilt experienced by the rebel sons of the primeval horde-father have been transmitted to their descendants and have been the basis of all subsequent religion ; while, on the contrary, the horror of incest (which is assumed to have been evoked in each generation during and since those remote ages) has not become in any degree innate.

Another serious difficulty arises in connexion with those forms of taboo known as ‘ avoidance customs ’, avoidance of females of the same totem, mothers-in-law, and so on. Freud assumes that the avoidance custom is evidence of unconscious incestuous desire: for only if the desire (and also horror of it as incestuous) be present will the avoidance taboo be maintained.

> If taboo expresses itself in prohibition it may well be considered self-evident . . . that it is based on a positive desireful impulse. For what nobody desires to do does not have to be forbidden (p. 117).

We have then to suppose that the incestuous desire for the mother is extended to all women who are 'objects of avoidance'. It would seem that this incestuous desire is a so highly inflammable passion that the mere acquisition by any woman of a position in any way resembling that of the mother (e.g., that of mother-in-law, or that of membership in the mother's totem group), suffices to direct it upon such a woman and thereby to necessitate the imposition of the taboo.

In these few critical remarks I have been willing to give Freud all the rope he asks for, and even more: but there are limits to our credulity beyond which even the glamour and prestige of the Freudian psychology cannot and should not carry us; and in this matter, I think, those limits have been passed.

I cannot conclude without citing one delicious example of the working of the Freudian imagination.

> With the introduction of agriculture the importance of the son in the patriarchal family increased. He was emboldened to give new expression to his incestuous *libido* which found symbolic satisfaction in labouring over mother earth (p. 253).

So that agriculture also can be traced back to the Oedipus complex. It is true that many anthropologists have shown reason to think that women were the first cultivators of the soil. But that difficulty can be swept away by the aid of a little imagination : no doubt these first female wielders of the spade were accustomed to speak of ' father earth ', and by so doing were enabled to secure the much-needed symbolic satisfaction of their incestuous *libido.* Further, is it not possible that men, when they speak of ' mother earth ', are really disguising the fact that unconsciously they regard the earth as their father, and that, when they thrust their implements into it, they are repeating the primordial tragedy of the slaying of their much-loved and much-hated father ? This suggestion may be recommended by the fact that its acceptance would at once explain the practice of earth-eating or geophagy which at one time may have been universal. It would also explain the universal tendency of boys to cover themselves with mud : for, if the earth is the father, it is obvious that mud is the blood of the father ; and that by thus imbruing their hands with the blood of the father, they would find satisfaction for their unconscious hatred of him.

In short, is it not obvious that, if we allowed ourselves the laxity of reasoning which is habitual to Freud and many of his disciples, and if we possessed his fertile ingenuity, there would be literally no limits to the possibilities of application of his principles, and that every detail of the conduct of men in all the seven ages might be traced back to the same foul root, ' the Oedipus complex ' ?

APPENDIX II

PROFESSOR FREUD'S GROUP PSYCHOLOGY AND HIS THEORY OF SUGGESTION

It is matter for rejoicing that the great leader of the psycho-analytic movement has of late years turned his attention to some of the deepest problems of social psychology. In so doing he brings his theories of human nature, built up through the study of individuals, to the test of their usefulness in wider fields, fields in which students who cannot claim to be psycho-analysts by profession may hope to weigh and to criticize them on a footing of equality. We are grateful to Professor Freud because, in thus coming out into the open, he grants us a taste of

> That stern joy which warriors feel
> In foemen worthy of their steel.

In an earlier article I have examined one of Professor Freud's contributions to Social Psychology.[1] In this place I propose to examine a more recent contribution, one which aims to go to the very roots of Group Psychology, namely, *Group Psychology and the Analysis of the Ego*.[2]

Professor Freud begins by pointing out that many writers on Social Psychology have been content to found

[1] The Review of *Totem and Taboo* in *Mind*.

[2] A translation of *Massenpsychologie und Ich-Analyse*, 1921, published by The International Psycho-analytical Press, 1922.

much of their construction on the postulate of a ' social instinct ' in man.

> But we may perhaps venture to object that it seems difficult to attribute to the factor of number a significance so great as to make it capable by itself of arousing in our mental life a new instinct that is otherwise not brought into play. Our expectation is, therefore, directed toward two other possibilities; that the social instinct may not be a primitive one and insusceptible of dissection, and that it may be possible to discover the beginnings of its development in a narrower circle, such as that of the family.

Having thus defined his goal, Professor Freud proceeds to examine the views of some other writers on the fundamentals of Group Psychology, more especially those of M. le Bon and of myself. He accepts le Bon's assertion that participation in the life of a ' psychological group ' profoundly modifies the thinking, feeling, and acting of the individual; and he asks:

> What, then, is a group? How does it acquire the capacity for exercising such a decisive influence over the mental life of the individual? And what is the nature of the mental change which it forces upon the individual? It is the task of a theoretical Group Psychology to answer these three questions.

Freud finds himself in substantial agreement with le Bon in respect of the peculiarities of the individual in the group.

> When individuals come together in a group, all their individual inhibitions fall away and all the cruel, brutal and destructive instincts, which lie dormant in individuals as relics of a primitive epoch, are stirred up to find free gratification.

And

> The apparently new characteristics which he [the individual] then displays are, in fact, the manifestations of this unconscious, in which all that is evil in the human mind is contained as a predisposition. We can find no difficulty in understanding the disappearance of conscience or of a sense of responsibility in these circumstances. It has long been our contention that 'dread of society (*Sociale Angst*)' is the essence of what is called conscience.

The captious critic might here interpose to ask—Why should conscience, if it is simply dread of society, disappear or cease to function just when a man is most thickly surrounded by the fellow-members of society?

Also, without captiousness, we may fairly ask for more definition of 'all the cruel, brutal and destructive instincts' which constitute the predisposition of all that is evil in the human mind.

In his later writings Professor Freud has no longer been content to postulate a single instinct, the sexual, but makes reference to a considerable array of instincts. These references excite in me the liveliest curiosity; a curiosity which seems doomed to remain unsatisfied. For my part, although since childhood I have been familiar with references, in sermons and popular addresses, to 'cruel, brutal and destructive instincts, which lie dormant in individuals as relics of a primitive epoch', I have always been sceptical as to the existence of such instincts in the human species; and the more I have studied the problems of instinct, the more has this scepticism hardened toward flat disbelief.

Perhaps it is unreasonable to demand consistency from so great a pioneer as Professor Freud: yet I will venture to point out that in another recent work (*Reflections on*

War and Death) Freud has asserted what I believe to be a truer doctrine:

> Psychological or, strictly speaking, psycho-analytical investigation, proves that . . . the deepest character of man consists of impulses of an elemental kind which are similar in all human beings, the aim of which is the gratification of certain primitive needs. These impulses are in themselves *neither good nor evil.*

Freud accepts le Bon's assertion of increased suggestibility of the crowd-member, rightly points out that le Bon leaves this fact entirely unexplained, and marks it down as a fundamental problem to be dealt with. He notes also, as two other important problems brought out by le Bon's descriptive account of crowds, the contagion of emotions and the prestige of leaders.

Freud (unlike le Bon, Sighele, Schallmeyer, Trotter, Martin, and most of the other writers who have dwelt upon the defects and ferocities of the crowd) is not blind to the fundamental paradox of group psychology, the paradox on which I have insisted in my *Group Mind*, namely, that, while immersion in the crowd commonly degrades the individual below his normal level, yet it is only by participation in group life that any man achieves his humanity and rises above the level of animal life: for, passing on to give in Chapter III an incomplete and brief *résumé* of my views, he recognizes this paradox as another fundamental problem. In my *Group Mind* I maintained that the solution of this problem is to be found in the organization of the group; that, in proportion as a group becomes organized, it gets rid of the peculiar defects and weaknesses of the crowd and becomes capable of higher modes of functioning and, under the better forms of organization, capable of raising its members rather than degrading them. But Freud seems to reject my explanation by organization, for he writes :

> It seems to us that the condition which McDougall designates as the 'organization' of a group can with more justification be described in another way. The problem consists in how to procure for the group precisely those features which were characteristic of the individual and which are extinguished in him by the formation of the group. For the individual, outside the primitive group, possessed his own continuity, his self-consciousness, his traditions and customs, his own particular functions and position, and kept apart from his rivals. Owing to his entry into an 'unorganized' group, he had lost this distinctiveness for a time.

But this is merely a restatement of the problem ; it suggests no alternative solution of it. Curiously enough, Freud, having recognized this problem and having implied that he has some alternative solution for it, passes on and does not, in the course of this book, return to it. He closes his reference to it with the following cryptic comment :

> If we thus recognize that the aim of the group is to equip the group with the attributes of the individual, we shall be reminded of a valuable remark of Trotter to the effect that the tendency towards the formation of groups is biologically a continuation of the multicellular character of all the higher organizations.

In this chapter Freud mentions also the principle I have invoked for the explanation of the intensified emotional reactions of crowds. He writes :

> The manner in which individuals are thus carried away by a common impulse is explained by McDougall by means of what he calls the 'principle of direct induction of emotion

by way of the primitive sympathetic response ', that is, by means of the emotional contagion with which we are already familiar.

Now, le Bon, fully recognizing the fact and the importance of emotional contagion in crowds, had treated it as one manifestation of suggestion. I, on the other hand, had treated it as a fundamental phenomenon, distinct from all the phenomena of suggestion and requiring a different explanation or theory. That explanation I had supplied in the theory of primitive passive sympathy or direct induction of emotion. In this I had been anticipated in some measure by Malebranche, as Dr. Drever has pointed out, but by no other writer. The theory is bound up with my view of the relation of the primary emotions to the instincts, and stands or falls with that view. The theory is based on a large array of facts of behaviour of the gregarious animals ; namely, that among such animals the display of any instinctive emotional reaction by one member of the species is apt to provoke similar instinctive emotional reactions in all other members of the species that perceive these reactions ; as when the behaviour of fear in one member of a flock provokes fear behaviour in other members. For the explanation of these facts, my theory assumes that each of the major instincts is so organized on its perceptual side that the expressions of the same instinct in other individuals of the species are effective provocatives of the instinct in the perceiving animal. And it postulates a similar special perceptual organization of the major instincts of the species *Homo sapiens*. Freud, in saying of my theory, ' that is, by means of the emotional contagion with which we are already familiar ', reduces my explanation to a mere restatement of the facts in generalized form.

It is true that we are all familiar with the facts of emotional contagion. The question is—have we any theory adequate to the explanation of them? The fact or phenomenon is one of the most fundamental with which a theoretical Group Psychology has to grapple. I have endeavoured to progress from the purely descriptive stage, represented by le Bon, to a theoretical explanation of the fact. Freud entirely overlooks my theory, in saying that I explain the fact 'by means of the emotional contagion with which we are already familiar'. I protest that I do not suffer from any such delusion as is here attributed to me by Professor Freud; the delusion, namely, that, in describing a large array of phenomena in general terms, I in any sense explain them. My theory of primitive passive sympathy is a perfectly definite and plausible theory for the explanation of the facts of emotional contagion; it is not a mere restatement of the facts in general terms. Let me illustrate the point by reference to laughter. Laughter is notoriously contagious. But why and how? We do not explain the fact by saying that it is a case of the emotional contagion with which we are already familiar. In saying that, we merely classify it with a wider group of similar phenomena. My theory is that the laughter instinct[1] (like most of the major instincts of man) is so innately organized on its receptive or perceptual side that the auditory and the visual perception of laughter excite the laughter instinct. If we seek any deeper or further explanation, we may plausibly suppose that these special perceptual adaptations of the instincts of the gregarious species have been produced in the course of

[1] Cp. my theory of laughter in *Outline of Psychology*, p. 165.

evolution, because they secure, among the members of any group, that emotional and impulsive congruity which is a principal foundation-stone of all group-life, animal and human. There is no rival theory in the field, so far as I know. Freud does not further deal with the problem, beyond implying that he agrees with le Bon in regarding emotional contagion as one of the manifestations 'so often covered by the enigmatic word "suggestion"'. And he proceeds in the following chapter to deal with the enigma of suggestion. In fact, the rest of the book is devoted to the elaboration of a theory of suggestion. He begins by insisting again on

the fundamental fact of Group Psychology—the two theses as to the intensification of the emotions and the inhibition of the intellect in primitive groups. Our interest is now directed to discovering the psychological explanation of this mental change which is experienced by the individual in a group.

It is clear, [says Freud] that rational factors . . . do not cover the observable phenomena. But what we are offered as an explanation by authorities upon Sociology and Group Psychology is always the same, even though it is given various names, and that is—the magic word 'suggestion'. Tarde calls it 'imitation'; but we cannot help agreeing with a writer who protests that imitation comes under the concept of suggestion, and is in fact one of its results. Le Bon traces back all the puzzling features of social phenomena to two factors: the mutual suggestion of individuals and the prestige of leaders. But prestige, again, is only recognizable by its capacity for evoking suggestion. McDougall for a moment gives us an impression that his principle of 'primitive induction of emotion' might enable us to do without the assumption of suggestion. But on further consideration we are forced to perceive that this principle says no more than the familiar assertions about 'imitation' or 'contagion', except for a decided stress upon the emotional factor.

Now, if Professor Freud had done me the honour to read my *Introduction to Social Psychology* (a thing which, so far as I can judge, neither he nor any one of his many disciples has ever done), instead of reading only my *Group Mind* (which is explicitly founded upon the other book and is essentially an attempt to apply to the problems of group psychology the principles arrived at in the earlier work), he would have seen that I distinguish clearly between suggestion and emotional contagion, and, further, that I have there propounded, not only a theory of emotional contagion, but also a distinct theory of suggestion. He would then not have committed the error of saying that there has been, during thirty years, no change in the situation as regards suggestion and that there has been no explanation of the nature of suggestion, that is, of the conditions under which influence without adequate logical foundation takes place.

Since Freud has thus entirely overlooked my theory of suggestion, I beg leave to restate it here, in order that the reader may compare it with the very complicated theory which is the main substance of Freud's book. My theory sets out from the fact of observation that, among animals of gregarious species, we commonly find relations of dominance and submission ; we see some members of a herd or flock submitting tamely and quietly to the dominance, the leadership, the self-assertion of other members. This submission does not always or commonly seem to imply fear. Yet it is unquestionably instinctive. I have argued, therefore, that such behaviour is the expression of a distinct and specific instinct of submission : an instinct which is apt to be evoked by the aggressive or self-assertive behaviour of other, especially larger and older, members of the group, and whose goal or function it is to secure harmony within the group by prompting the junior and weaker members of it to submit to the leadership of others, to follow them, to ' knuckle under to them ' without protest, to accept their slightest word as law, to feel humble or lowly in their presence and to adopt lowly or ' crestfallen ' attitudes before them. My theory maintains that the human species also is endowed with this instinct of submission; and that, with the development of language and intellect, verbal indications of the attitudes of the strong become very important means of evoking and directing this submissive impulse; that this impulse, the emotional conative tendency of this instinct, is the main conative factor at work in all instances of true suggestion, whether waking or hypnotic. Further, that, in human societies, reputation for power of any sort becomes a very important factor in evoking this impulse, supplementing and, in fact, largely supplanting, the bodily evidences of superior powers which, on the animal plane, are the principal excitants of this impulse; such reputation constituting the essence of all that we call prestige, the power of using suggestion, of compelling bodily and mental obedience or docility, without evoking fear. My theory maintains that, if the human species were not gregarious, and if its native constitution did not comprise also this special submissive instinct, human beings would not be suggestible; and, therefore, the social life of man would be profoundly other than it is.[1]

[1] I say that this instinct of submission is evidenced by the animals of many gregarious species. But I maintain that it is distinct from the gregarious instinct itself; that there are species of animals which have the gregarious instinct, but lack the submissive instinct; just as there are men who are strongly gregarious, but in whom the submissive instinct operates very little, if at all; that is to say, I maintain that

Freud and his disciples make frequent reference to ego-instincts; but they have never, so far as I know, attempted to define these postulated ego-instincts. I imagine that, if they would undertake to attempt to define them, it would appear that these ego-instincts are identical with what I have attempted to distinguish and define as two distinct instincts, the instincts of self-assertion and of submission. But Freud does not seek in the ego-instincts the explanation of suggestion. Rather his theory of suggestion is very much more complex. I will try to sketch it briefly and fairly.

Freud's theory of suggestion derives all the phenomena of suggestion from his *libido*. '*Libido* is an expression taken from the theory of the emotions. We call by that name the energy (regarded as a quantitative magnitude, though not at present actually measurable) of those instincts which have to do with all that may be comprised under the word "love".'

Then comes a passage, in which Freud seeks to justify once more his acceptance of the popular usage of the word 'love' as evidence of the essential unity of all manifestations to which the word 'love' can with any propriety be applied, including, besides sexual attraction or lust, 'on the one hand, self-love, and on the other love for parents and children, friendship and love for humanity in general, and also devotion to concrete

the gregarious and the submissive tendencies are independent variables and, therefore, cannot be properly ascribed to the same instinct. In this I dissent strongly from the teaching of Mr. Wilfred Trotter, who, throughout his famous little book on *Instincts of the Herd in Peace and War*, assumes without question that all the phenomena commonly classed under the head of suggestion are sufficiently explained by invoking the 'herd instinct'.

objects and to abstract ideas '. He goes on to say : ' We will try our fortune, then, with the supposition that love relationships (or, to use a more neutral expression, emotional ties) also constitute the essence of the group mind.' He adds : ' Let us remember that the authorities made no mention of any such relations. What would correspond to them is evidently concealed behind the shelter, the screen, of suggestion.'

Freud then proceeds to the study of highly-organized groups and especially churches and armies ; for, as he says, ' the most interesting examples of such structures are churches—communities of believers—and armies '. He finds common to them one essential feature, namely, ' the same illusion holds good of there being a head—in the Catholic Church, Christ ; in any army its Commander-in-Chief—who loves all the individuals in the group with an equal love. Everything depends upon this illusion ; if it were to be dropped, then both Church and army would dissolve, so far as external force permitted them to '. To all the members of the Church, Christ is ' their father surrogate ' ; and to all the members of an army, the Commander-in-Chief is their father surrogate. In the latter case the relation is multiplied by the official hierarchy :

> Every Captain is, as it were, the Commander-in-Chief and the father of his company, and so is every non-commissioned officer of his section.
>
> It is to be noticed that in these two artificial groups each individual is bound by libidinal ties on the one hand to the leader . . . and on the other hand to the other members of the group. . . . It would appear as though we were on the right road toward an explanation of the principal phenomenon of Group Psychology—the individual's lack of freedom in the group. If each individual is bound in two directions by

such an intense emotional tie, we shall find no difficulty in attributing to that circumstance the alteration and limitation which have been observed in his personality.

Precisely! *If* the individual is so bound, and, given the protean nature of the *libido*, anything may follow, any phenomena of group life may with a little ingenuity be attributed to these alleged libidinous ties. But the question remains—Are these ties really there in all groups? Are they really the fundamental factors of all group life? Or are they merely asserted to be there by Professor Freud, in order to make Group Psychology a mere annex of his psycho-analytic system?

Freud finds in the panic evidence of the truth of his view. He would distinguish between collective fear and true panic. He writes:

> The contention that dread in a group is increased to enormous proportions by means of induction (contagion) is not in the least contradicted by these remarks. McDougall's view meets the case entirely when the danger is a really great one and when the group has no strong emotional ties—conditions which are fulfilled, for instance, when a fire breaks out in a theatre or a place of amusement.[1]

---

[1] Freud's theory compels him to make this distinction between collective fear and the true panic; for he can hardly ask us to believe that *all* the members of every theatre audience are bound together by strong libidinous ties, nor can he hope to persuade us that *all* the members of every such audience are dominated by a common father surrogate special to the occasion. Yet every such assembly is liable to collective fear. It is, perhaps, worth while to point out that Freud makes no attempt to show that there is any difference between the phenomena of the collective fear and of the panic; as there surely should be, if these are two distinct and differently conditioned manifestations.

But he contends that in a body of troops panic may break out under conditions no more threatening than others which they have encountered without disorder; and that in these cases the essential condition of this, the true panic, as distinguished from mere collective fear, is the death of the leader.

Now, if this new theory of the panic is true, there must have occurred during the late war a multitude of such panics; and we might fairly demand that Freud should support his theory by the citation of one or two authentic accounts of such panics induced by the death of leaders. But we find no such citations. In place of them we are offered in evidence only a scene from a play; or rather not even from a play, but from a parody of a play.

> The typical occasion of the outbreak of a panic is very much as it is represented in Nestroy's parody of Hebbel's play about Judith and Holofernes—a soldier cries out: "The General has lost his head!" and thereupon all the Assyrians take to flight.

Freud adds:

> Anyone who, like McDougall, describes a panic as one of the plainest functions of the 'group mind' arrives at the paradoxical position that this group mind does away with itself in one of its most striking manifestations.

In answer to this, I would point out that I do not ascribe a group mind to a crowd, nor do I regard a panic as a function of the group mind; the panic is rather a function of an instinct operating in an unorganized group. I admit that the death of a leader may contribute to bring about a panic; but I submit that the grounds of this are sufficiently obvious, that it requires no far-fetched theories for its explanation. The reasoning of Freud's paragraphs, following those in which he treats of panics, shows that his theory requires that, on the death of the leader, the group shall break out, not into panic, but into an orgy of mutual murder. For, he tells us, it is only the libidinous ties between the leader and the members and those between the members (which latter *somehow* are derivative from the former) which keep in check our narcissism; and narcissism is ruthless murderous self-seeking. That this, rather than panic, is the consequence of the death of the leader logically demanded by Freud's theory is clearly shown by his next section, which deals with the religious group.

'The dissolution of a religious group is not so easy *to observe*' (italics mine). And so here also Freud turns to literature and finds his evidence in a story which, if not a parody of a story, is little more, namely, the notorious sensational novel *When It Was Dark*. This novel, which achieved a great popular success, is offered us as evidence, because it was recommended by the Bishop of London, and because 'it gave a clever and, as it seems to me, a convincing picture of such a possibility and its consequences'. The whole passage deserves citation:

The novel, which is supposed to relate to the present day, tells how a conspiracy of enemies to the figure of Christ and of the Christian faith succeeds in arranging for a sepulchre to be discovered in Jerusalem. In this sepulchre is an inscription, in which Joseph of Arimathea confesses that for reasons of piety he secretly removed the body of Christ from its grave on the third day after its entombment and buried it in this spot. The resurrection of Christ and His divine nature are by this means disposed of, and the result of this archaeological discovery is a convulsion in European civilization and an extraordinary increase in all crimes and acts of violence, which only ceases when the forgers' plot has been revealed.

The phenomenon which accompanies the dissolution that is here supposed to overtake a religious group *is not dread*, for which the occasion is wanting. Instead of it, ruthless and hostile impulses toward other people make their appearance, which, owing to the equal love of Christ, they had previously been unable to do.[1]

In the next chapter Freud briefly recognizes the existence of leaderless groups. These, which might be supposed to offer some serious difficulty to a theory which makes the leader the centre of all group-ties, he brushes lightly aside with the suggestion that an idea, an abstraction, or even a common wish, may serve as a substitute for a leader, as an object or centre for our libidinous impulses.

Having arrived at the view that libidinous ties are constitutive of every group, Freud very properly turns to being-in-love in the ordinary sense of the words, in order to study the phenomena more intimately; and here he finds ' identification ' to be the centre of interest. ' Identification is the earliest and original form of emotional tie.' It culminates in the cannibal, who,

> as we know, has remained at this standpoint; he has a devouring affection for his enemies and only devours people of whom he is fond.

There follows an intricate discussion of love, in the course of which the *ego* and the ego-ideal and other entities spring back and forth between the self and the object, the object becoming the self and the self the

[1] It happens that I have some slight acquaintance with the author of this precious story, and I venture to think that he would be immensely tickled to know that his successful effort to boil the domestic pot is now seriously cited as evidence in support of a scientific theory.

object, in a manner so puzzling to any but a hardened believer, that I can make out of it only the following: Freud recognizes, as I have done, two principle factors in normal sexual love, sensuality or lust on the one hand, tenderness on the other: but, whereas I have identified these two factors of sexual love with the impulse of the sex-instinct and the impulse of the parental or protective instinct, respectively, Freud feels himself bound to derive both of them from the sexual *libido*. He describes the tender factor as a part of the sexual impulse inhibited in its aim. By what influence this part is supposed to be inhibited is not very clear. Nor is it clear why, being inhibited, its nature should be transformed into its opposite. The natural result of obstruction to the sexual instinct would seem to be, as in all other cases, anger, as we see in animals. However, granting this miraculous transformation into tenderness of one-half of the *libido*, we then have sexual love consisting essentially in one-half of the sexual *libido* working toward its sexual goal, but restrained by the other half, which, by inhibition, has been transformed into its opposite, tenderness. How much simpler to recognize (in accordance with a wealth of facts of human and animal behaviour and in conflict with none) that parental care is primarily the expression of a special instinct independent of and quite different from the sexual instinct; and to see in sexual love the play of these two impulses reciprocally modifying one another, and modified still further in most cases by other equally independent tendencies!

Freud seeks further light on love from hypnosis:

From being in love to hypnosis is evidently only a short step—the hypnotic relation is the devotion of someone in love to an unlimited degree, but with sexual satisfaction excluded . . . But, on the other hand, we may also say that the hypnotic relation is (if the expression is permissible) a group formation with two members. . . . Hypnosis is distinguished from a group formation by this limitation of number, just as it is distinguished from being in love by the absence of directly sexual tendencies. In this respect it occupies a middle position between the two.

Hypnosis contains, then, the key to the crowd. The reader at this point in the book begins to think he is near the end of his journey. A group is a crowd hypnotized by its leader ; and to be hypnotized is to be in love, to have one's sexual *libido* fixated upon the hypnotizer in two halves, one half inhibited, the other half uninhibited. The group is a crowd in love with its leader ; and suggestibility is a consequence of being in love.

But Freud rightly recognizes that the explanation of suggestion is not so simple as this account implies.

There is still a great deal in it which we must recognize as unexplained and mystical. It contains an additional element of paralysis derived from the relation between someone with superior power and someone who is without power and helpless.

So the indefatigable Freud sets off on another tack to find the grounds of this further unexplained and mystical element in suggestion. He begins by examining Mr. Trotter's view, which finds the explanation of all suggestion in the herd instinct. He rejects this view on the grounds, first, that ' it can be made at all events probable that the herd instinct is not irreducible, that it is not primary in the same sense as the instinct of self-preservation and the sexual instinct '. Secondly, on the ground that it explains the group, without assigning an essential place or function to a leader ; and Freud has already asserted that the leader is the essential key to the group. Freud then makes the following astonishing *tour de force*, and brings us back to the original position from which he set out.

> *Gemeingeist*, *esprit de corps*, 'group spirit', &c., does not belie its derivation from what was originally envy. . . . Social justice means that we deny ourselves many things so that others may have to do without them as well, or, what is the same thing, may not be able to ask for them. This demand for equality is the root of social conscience and the sense of duty.[1]

But what then is envy, which is thus identified with a demand for equality and as the root of all the social virtues ? Is envy the expression of some special instinct ? No, its explanation is to be found in the fact that man is not, as Trotter asserts, a herd animal, but 'rather a horde animal, an individual creature in a horde led by a chief'. Now, the characteristics of a crowd imply regression of its members 'to a primitive mental activity, of just such a sort as we should be inclined to ascribe to the primal horde. Thus the group appears to us as a revival of the primal horde. Just as primitive man virtually survives in every individual, so the primal horde may arise once more out of any random crowd.'

Thus the long trail leads back to 'Totem and Taboo' and the horde-father. This primal superman 'had pre-

[1] The reader should notice here that, according to this strange doctrine, the group spirit and social justice alike are founded in, or are expressions of, an attitude considerably meaner and more despicable than that of the dog in the manger ! The dog in the manger says—'You shall not eat, because I cannot eat !' According to Freud, the socially just man's attitude essentially is—'I will not eat, in order that I may have the pleasure of preventing you from eating.'

vented his sons from satisfying their directly sexual tendencies; he forced them into abstinence and consequently into the emotional ties with him and with one another which could arise out of those of their tendencies that were inhibited in their sexual aim. He forced them, so to speak, into group psychology. His sexual jealousy and intolerance became in the last resort the causes of group psychology.' Now we see why, in the opening chapter, Freud wrote of *the illusion* that is the prime condition of all group-life, the illusion on the part of the members that they are equally loved by the leader. For the primal horde-father does not love his sons; he is merely consumed and motivated by sexual jealousy against them. 'The illusion that the leader loves all of the individuals equally and justly . . . is simply an idealistic remodelling of the state of affairs in the primal horde, where all of the sons knew that they were equally persecuted by the primal father, and feared him equally'; and where the primal father, by forbidding them all sexual gratification, forced them to love him and to love one another. This is described as a process of 'recasting upon which all social duties are built up'.

This same recasting process explains 'what is still incomprehensible and mysterious in group formations—all that lies hidden behind the enigmatic words "hypnosis" and "suggestion"'.

Let us recall that hypnosis has something positively uncanny about it; but the characteristic of uncanniness suggests something old and familiar that has undergone repression. Let us consider how hypnosis is induced. The hypnotist asserts that he is in possession of a mysterious power which robs the subject of his own will, or, which is the same thing, the subject believes it of him. This mysterious power . . . must be the same that is looked upon by primitive people as the source of taboo, the same that emanates from kings and chieftains, and makes it dangerous to approach them (*mana*). The hypnotist, then, is supposed to be in possession of this power; and how does he manifest it? By telling the subject to look him in the eyes; his most typical method of hypnotizing is by his look. But it is precisely the sight of the chieftain that is dangerous and unbearable for primitive people, just as later that of the Godhead is for mortals.

By the measures that he takes, then, the hypnotist awakens in the subject a portion of his archaic inheritance which had also made him compliant towards his parents. . . . What is thus awakened is the idea of a paramount and dangerous personality, toward whom only a passive-masochistic attitude is possible, toward whom one's will has to be surrendered . . . the uncanny and coercive characteristics of group formations, which are shown in their suggestion phenomena, may therefore with justice be traced back to the fact of their origin from the primal horde. The leader of the group is still the dreaded primal father; the group still wishes to be governed by unrestricted force; it has an extreme passion for authority; in le Bon's phrase, it has a thirst for obedience.[1] The primal father is the group ideal, which governs the ego in the place of the ego-ideal. Hypnotism has a good claim to being described as a group of two; there remains as a definition for suggestion . . . a conviction which is not based upon perception and reasoning but upon an erotic tie.

---

[1] How or why the persecuted sons of the primal horde-father acquire a passion for being persecuted is nowhere explained. Even if we accept Freud's dictum that to 'persecute a man and to force him to deny himself all sexual gratification is the surest way to earn his love,' it is not obvious that the victim will at the same time develop a passionate desire to be persecuted, or that he will transmit this desire to his remote descendants.

Further :

> we have come to the conclusion that suggestion is a partial manifestation of the state of hypnosis, and that hypnosis is solidly founded upon a *predisposition which has survived in the unconscious from the early history of the human family.*[1]

Here we have come to the end of the long and tortuous trail, and have found as the root of all social psychology an ancient disposition impressed upon the race[2] (or rather upon the male half of it) by its experiences during the period of life in the primal horde under the dominance of a brutal horde-father; the disposition thus acquired by the species makes men docile, obedient, suggestible to all who manifest superior power and prestige. Freud further assumes that the same disposition makes men desire to be led, dominated, commanded, bullied, and further, makes them love those that persecute them and at the same time love their fellow victims of persecution. The remainder of the book restates some of the positions reached and deals with some other hardly related problems.

Let me try to summarize the complex theory as fairly as possible in a few lines. The main factor in group

[1] The phrase in italics clearly shows that the theory of suggestion reached by Freud in this book is essentially identical with the theory first propounded by me in 1908 and restated more fully in my *Note on Suggestion* of 1920. All that Freud has added is the complicated and highly speculative story of the phylogenetic differentiation from the sex instinct of the innate disposition whose impulse is (according to our common theory) the essential dynamic factor in all successful suggestion.

[2] That is, to say, an instinctive disposition to obey, split off or differentiated from the sex-instinct by the horde-father's bullying and developed in Lamarckian fashion.

life is suggestion. The fundamental problem of Group Psychology, therefore, is the nature of suggestion. Suggestion is always of the same nature as the suggestion of hypnosis; and the study of hypnosis shows that suggestion depends upon a peculiar emotional attitude of the patient to the hypnotizer. This attitude results from the reanimation (by regression) of an atavistic survival, an innate disposition to submission acquired by the race during the long period in which men lived in the primal horde, a horde dominated by a brutal horde-leader fiercely jealous of his sexual rights over all the women. This horde-leader forced all his fellow-males to repress their sexual urgings; their repressed *libido* then became fixated on him, so that they loved him, and falsely believed that he loved them, at the same time that they feared him for his brutal domination and plotted to slay him. When any man lives as a member of a group and is subject to group influences, when he accepts the traditional morality and develops the virtues of the good and patriotic citizen, it is because some leader throws him back from his hard-won individuality, forces upon him an atavistic regression to the complex attitude proper toward the leader of the primitive horde, so that he becomes suggestible toward him; but the part of the leader may be played by an abstract idea, or even by a wish or aspiration held in common by a number of individuals.

What verdict shall be given upon this story of the phylogenesis of the submissive disposition? First, it may be said, if there were no other explanations of the facts of group life, we should have to entertain it seriously. But, as I have endeavoured to show, other simpler, less extravagant, explanations are possible and are at least as adequate.

Secondly, the attempt to make the theory of suggestion (together with all the peculiar Freudian assumptions upon which it is based) explain all the facts of group-life leaves many obscure problems. For example, it leaves the leaderless group unexplained; for we can hardly take seriously the assertion that an abstract idea or a wish may play the role assigned to the leader in forcing regression to the atavistic attitude. It leaves untouched the fact that women are at least as suggestible as men, and probably on the whole more so: we shall have to invent some other story to account for their suggestibility. It leaves very obscure the suggestibility of the members of a group toward one another. Here I would especially cite such instances as the famous spread of the rumour of Russian troops passing through England in the autumn of 1914. It is impossible to point in such instances to a leader. We must be content to suppose this to be an instance where a wish played the role of leader. But is not this equivalent to rejecting the theory of the leader as the *sine qua non* of all group phenomena? Further, it does not explain the primary fact of contagion of emotion, so fundamental to all group-life. And it does not explain how a leader attains leadership; how he manages to force regression upon his followers and to constitute himself a leader.

Finally, it reduces all the social life of men, including all team-work, all patriotism, all moral self-control and discipline, all self-sacrifice for the good of the community, to the working of an atavistic regression, to a return to the behaviour proper to the (very hypothetical) remote age in which the violence of a bully, armed with a club and prompted by sexual jealousy, was the only controlling force in human society. It makes sexual jealousy and envy the roots of all the nobler manifestations of human life. Yet it leaves these roots themselves unexplained. Why jealousy? Why envy? If the sexual impulse, the fear of death, and the urge for food, were the whole of the instinctive endowment of primitive man, why should not the primal horde have enjoyed a delightful promiscuity? On that plane one woman can serve many men. We should expect sexual jealousy, if anywhere, only among the women.

My verdict is 'not proven and wildly improbable'. If we positively knew, if by any supernatural unchallenge-able authority we were assured, that all the phenomena of human life, all the modes of human activity, had been derived from sexuality, and must be explained as manifestations of the sexual *libido*, we might be induced to say that Professor Freud's theory of social phenomena in general was a most ingenious and praiseworthy effort to solve an insoluble problem.[1]

But we have no such guarantee. The only authority we have for accepting this as the necessary and sole permissible line of speculation, for regarding our explanations of social phenomena as necessarily confined within the limits of the sexual *libido*, is the authority of Professor Freud and of his devoted disciples. I, for one, shall continue to try to avoid the spell of the primal horde-father and to use what intellect I have, untrammelled by arbitrary limitations.

[1] What I am here rejecting is Freud's theory that the tendency to submit and obey is derived from or differentiated from the sexual instinct and in the complicated fashion imagined by him. That the human species, like many others, is endowed with such an innate tendency, and that all successful suggestions bring this tendency into play as the essential conative factor of the response of the suggestee to the suggestor, that is the essence of my theory of suggestion (as it is of Freud's).

APPENDIX III

A GREAT ADVANCE OF THE FREUDIAN PSYCHOLOGY[1]

It is interesting to find that Professor Freud is less rigidly Freudian than many of his ardent disciples. Readers of Freudian literature will remember how in 1919 a group of Freudians (*Zur Psycho-analyse der Kriegsneurosen*—with introduction by Professor Freud) endeavoured to show that the neuroses of the war might be interpreted in terms of the Freudian principles. In spite of much ingenuity the endeavour can hardly have seemed successful to any impartial reader. More recently Professor Freud himself has frankly abandoned this attempt. In his *Beyond the Pleasure-Principle*, he acknowledges that further consideration of the war-cases has led him to profound modifications of his theory. The recurrent war-dream has very naturally been a difficult problem for those who would bring it within the range of Freudian principles. In order to do this, it was necessary to make it appear that the fear, which was so prominent a feature of the war-dream, was somehow a sexual derivative and that somehow, in some sense, the patient was feeling or attaining pleasure through his torturing battle-dreams. Freud has now frankly abandoned this endeavour, and has modified his theory in the following way.

[1] Reprinted from *The Journal of Abnormal and Social Psychology*, vol. xx. 1945.

The original Freudian theory was a strange mixture (it could not be called a blend) of three irreconcilable principles, each of which is the fundamental assumption of a distinctive type of psychology, namely, first, mechanistic determinism; second, psychological hedonism (implied in a thorough-going sense by 'the pleasure-principle'); third, the hormic principle which sees the roots of all activities in instinctive urges, the primary prompters and sustainers of all thought and all action.

The phrase 'beyond the pleasure-principle' is now used by Freud to announce that he now recognizes the primacy of the hormic principle, the principle that instinctive urges work within us in relative independence of pleasure and pain. In this book Freud even comes near to recognizing that pleasure and pain are conditioned by the instinctive urgings, by their success and failure, and by their conflicts.

It is true that in an obscure way Freud has long recognized the inadequacy of the pleasure-principle and has embodied this recognition in a profoundly obscure term, namely, 'the reality-principle'. This was held to be a sort of interloper whose agency could be invoked whenever the pleasure-principle was too obviously out of the picture.

We know that the pleasure-principle is adjusted to a primary mode of operation on the part of the psychic apparatus, and that for the preservation of the organism amid the difficulties of the external world it is *ab initio* useless and indeed extremely dangerous. Under the influence of the instinct of the ego for self-preservation, it is replaced by the 'reality-principle'; which, without giving up the intention of ultimately attaining pleasure, yet demands and enforces the postponement of satisfaction, the renunciation of manifold possibilities of it, and the temporary endurance of ' pain ' on the long and circuitous road to pleasure.

And in the following passage, he seems to recognize, in a partial and grudging manner, the truth that pleasure and pain are conditioned by and upon our hormic or instinctive strivings:

It is at the same time indubitable that the replacement of the pleasure-principle by the reality-principle can account only for a small part, and that not the most intense, of painful experiences. Another and no less regular source of ' pain ' proceeds from the conflicts and dissociation in the psychic apparatus during the development of the ego towards a more highly co-ordinated organization. . . . The two sources of ' pain ' here indicated still do not nearly cover the majority of our painful experiences. . . . Most of the ' pain ' we experience is of the perceptual order, perception either of the urge of unsatisfied instincts or of something in the external world which may be painful in itself or may arouse painful anticipations in the psychic apparatus and is recognized by it as ' danger '. The reaction to these claims of impulse and these threats of danger, a reaction in which the real activity of the psychic apparatus is manifested, may be guided correctly by the pleasure-principle or by the reality-principle which modifies this. It seems thus unnecessary to recognize a still more far-reaching limitation of the pleasure-principle, and nevertheless it is precisely the investigation of the psychic reaction to external danger that may supply new material and new questions in regard to the problem here treated.

Freud then goes on to recognize that the pleasure-principle is not fundamental, that there is in us something deeper than or prior to the pleasure-principle, or, as I should put it, that pleasure and pain do but modify, in the way of promoting or checking, the fundamental urges of our instinctive nature. I do not say that Freud actually attains to this position ; rather, recognizing that something is more fundamental than pleasure as a determinant of activity, he invents a new and primary instinct which he calls ' the repetition-compulsion '.

Contemplating the obstinate recurrence of war-dreams and allied repeated manifestations of strong primary urges, Freud proposes to recognize as the most fundamental tendency of our nature a ' repetition-compulsion '.

> The new and remarkable fact, however, that we have now to describe is that the repetition-compulsion also revives experiences of the past that contain no potentiality of pleasure, and which could at no time have been satisfactory, even of impulses since repressed.

Again,

> It is a question naturally of the action of impulses that should lead to satisfaction, but the experience that instead of this they even then brought ' pain ' has borne no result. The act is repeated in spite of everything ; a powerful compulsion insists on it. . . . In the light of such observations as these, drawn from the behaviour during transference and from the fate of human beings, we may venture to make the assumption that there really exists in psychic life a repetition-compulsion, which goes beyond the pleasure-principle. We shall now also feel disposed to relate to this compelling force the dreams of shock-patients and the play-impulse of children.
>
> This (the repetition-compulsion) seems to us more primitive, more elementary, more instinctive than the pleasure-principle which is displaced by it—to which we have heretofore ascribed the domination over the course of the processes of excitation in the psychic life.

After making this great step towards a truer psychology, Freud sets out upon a highly speculative inquiry into the nature and origin of the repetition-compulsion and finds the explanation of it in the astonishing conclusion that all instincts, except the sexual, tend or strive toward death.

They (the instinctive tendencies) thus present the delusive appearance of forces striving after change and progress, while they are merely endeavouring to reach an old goal by ways both old and new. This final goal of all organic striving can be stated too. It would be counter to the conservative nature of instinct if the goal of life were a state never hitherto reached. It must rather be an ancient starting-point, which the living being left long ago, and to which it harks back again by the circuitous path of development. If we may assume as an experience admitting of no exception that everything living dies from causes within itself, and returns to the inorganic, we can only say 'The goal of all life is death', and, casting back, 'the inanimate was there before the animate'.

This highly characteristic piece of reasoning, with its strange conclusion, is hardly one that compels assent. There is surely a very much simpler explanation of all the facts which Freud explains by means of his 'repetition-compulsion'. They all follow naturally from our fundamental assumption, if that assumption is the validity of the hormic principle. According to this principle every instinctive tendency is a tendency towards a goal of a particular kind, and however it be brought into play it tends towards that goal. Hence repetition is of the essential nature of instinctive activity. The repetitive character appears, it is true, most strikingly in those instances in which by repression and dissociation a complex has been formed, especially in the case of relatively simple complexes that are completely dissociated: for in such a complex some strong instinctive tendency, bound up with some dissociated memory, works without the guidance of the personality which would modify its manifestations upon each occasion. Therefore in these cases we get such striking repetition-phenomena as the fugue, the fit, the phobia, the terror-dream, the battle-dream, the tic, the obsession or the compulsive act, the recurrent nausea, &c.

What need then to follow Freud in his extravagant speculation leading to the conclusion that all our instincts (except the sexual) including the food-seeking instinct and the instinct of fear or self-preservation, strive toward death ?

Freud asserts in the course of his discussion—' No knowledge would have been so important for the establishment of a sound psychology as some approximate understanding of the common nature and possible differences of the instincts.' This is the thesis on which I have not ceased to insist since writing my *Social Psychology* in 1907, and I venture to think that if Professor Freud and his followers had taken it to heart from the first, we should have seen more rapid advance, with less of misdirected ingenuity proposing impossible explanations under the misguidance of a false dogma, the dogma of the all-dominance of the pleasure-principle, which is nothing other than the long-discredited theory of psychological hedonism.

Freud and his followers, instead of attempting to define the human instincts, in the light of comparative psychology, instead of seeking what Freud now recognizes to be ' so important for the establishment of a sound psychology ', namely, ' some approximate understanding of the common nature and possible differences on the instincts ', have been content to postulate two groups of instincts, namely, sex-instincts and ego-instincts. They have been much concerned with the ontogenesis and phylogenesis of the former, but have been content to leave the latter group wholly undefined and unexplored. In addition Freud has occasionally made passing references to base instincts of cruelty, of destruction, or what not, without pausing further to define these.

The greatest need of present-day psychology is the incorporation with the hormic psychology, which has remained from Aristotle onward the soundest and most fruitful type of psychology, of all the valuable insight into human nature which the psycho-analytic movement and the genius of Freud have brought us. Freud's fundamental change of doctrine revealed in his *Beyond the Pleasure-Principle* is a most welcome step in this direction. It clears the way by repudiating a dogmatic error that has hitherto perverted all Freudian reasoning; and it sets the hormic principle solidly in the place of prime importance from which the pleasure-principle has been dethroned. But I do not believe that the mere regrouping of the sex-instinct or instincts and the ego-instincts, as respectively life-instincts and death-instincts, will serve to carry us appreciably nearer the much-to-be-desired goal, 'some approximate understanding of the common nature and possible differences of the instincts' as the essential foundation for 'the establishment of a sound psychology'.

In conclusion I would repeat that progress in our knowledge of the instincts of man is not to be achieved by exclusive psycho-analytic study of nervously deranged patients. Valuable as such studies are, they need to be supplemented by and correlated with the results of wide comparative study of men and animals. When we take such a wide standpoint, does not the Freudian attempt to display such instinctive reactions as fear and curiosity as in some sense disguised expressions of the sex-instinct, do not all such attempts appear as unbalanced and trivial exercises of minds narrowly confined to one small part of the whole vast field that invites the attention of the psychologist ?

APPENDIX IV

THE OEDIPUS COMPLEX

AN ATTEMPT TO ESTIMATE ITS ROLE AND IMPORTANCE [1]

I SHALL attempt to diminish in some degree the theoretical differences, familiar to all, by which students of human nature are so widely divided. Of all these divisions, the most regrettable seems to be that which has arisen between those who follow the banner of Professor Freud and those of us who cannot accept a large part of the teachings of that great pioneer. Among the several distinctive features of the Freudian psychology, the theory of the Oedipus complex is, I think, chiefly responsible for the continuance of the chasm that divides us. I shall attempt, therefore, to show that, although there is a certain amount of truth in the theory of the Oedipus complex, the range of influence of this complex has been grossly exaggerated in much of the Freudian literature. The success of such an attempt would materially diminish the width of the chasm in question.

Differences of opinion, even on fundamental problems of human nature, are inevitable and are, perhaps, necessary to the progress of our science; yet differences so deep and so acute as those which mark off the Freudian

[1] A paper read at the Fifty-First Annual Meeting of the American Neurological Association, Washington, D.C., May 1925, and here reprinted from the *Archives of Neurology and Psychiatry*, Vol. 15, with the kind permission of the editor.

group are unhealthy; they retard progress; they tend to bring all our science, all psychology, into disrepute with the lay public; for they seem to the educated public to mark it as a field of pseudo-science with no solid achievement to its credit, no common body of principles, no truths of permanent value, no knowledge that can be accepted as a sure guide in the perplexities of practical life.

Such a state of affairs would be regrettable in any science; but it is peculiarly unfortunate in psychology, the science of human behaviour, for two reasons: 1. Psychology is a science in which all men are more or less interested, to which men of the most varied callings are looking more and more for guidance. 2. It is a science in which the evaluation of evidence and the choice of principles is so difficult that a consensus of experts is absolutely necessary for the guidance of the lay public. In many of the sciences it is possible for a single worker to make a discovery, and to establish it by evidence so clear and decisive that the new truth is at once accepted by all his colleagues and by the public in general. In psychology this is not possible; every observation is capable of widely different interpretations, between which only experts can decide; and in the absence of any consensus of opinion among them, the public must continue to oscillate vaguely, likely to be inflated by each new wind of doctrine, seeking in vain any established principles of human nature which it may confidently apply to the urgent problems of daily living.

The chasm which I have pointed to as the most regrettable, that between the Freudians and the rest of us, is maintained and accentuated by both sides. Both sides are to blame. The Freudians regard us as blinded to their new revelation by our complexes. We retort by treating them as fanatical and credulous disciples of a false prophet. The result is a deadlock very difficult to resolve; yet resolved it must be. It will not be resolved by the unconditional capitulation of either party. I am convinced that it can be resolved only by mutual concessions, to be achieved by more sympathetic consideration by either party of the arguments of the other.

PART OF FREUDIAN PSYCHOLOGY ACCEPTED BY AUTHOR

Let me, then, say at once that according to my view there is much in Freud's psychology that is true and of fundamental importance. It is, I would maintain, right in recognizing (1) that human nature and behaviour are always and everywhere purposive, conative, hormic;[1]

[1] Whether this truth, fundamental for all psychology, can be reconciled with a strictly mechanistic view of the world is a deep question which we, as psychologists, may leave unanswered. But that the life of man is a series of strivings toward goals, near or remote, that these strivings are deeply rooted in his inmost constitution, is a truth which cannot be ignored by any psychology that aspires to practical usefulness. There are two distinct theories of these strivings. The hedonic theory asserts that they are efforts to obtain pleasure or avoid pain. The hormic theory maintains that they arise prior to and independently of experiences of pleasure and pain, which experiences are incidental to and secondary to our strivings, being determined respectively by the success or failure of our own efforts. It asserts that we strive to attain certain goals because it is our inborn nature so to strive; that we can in any sense explain these tendencies only by tracing the genesis of them in the evolutionary history of the species. In his earlier writings, Freud assumed the truth of both these theories, placing the hormic and the hedonic principles (or, as he calls them, 'the reality principle' and 'the pleasure principle') side by side as equally fundamental.

(2) that the mind is built up on a foundation of innate dispositions or instincts which, throughout our lives, prompt us all alike to seek certain natural goals, generating tendencies which rough-hew our ends, shape them as we may. (3) It is right in regarding these instinctive dispositions as springs of energy, energy that can be expressed in a multitude of varied activities, according to the principle which I defined more than thirty years ago as the vicarious usage of nervous or psychophysical energy. (4) It is right in regarding many disorders of both mind and body as arising from maladjustment of these hormic impulses, from conflict between them and from repression, resulting in the formation of morbid complexes, and from the continued subconscious workings of impulses thus repressed. (5) It is right in maintaining that these disorders can be prevented only by a better understanding of our instinctive nature and the modes of its operation, and can be cured only (in many cases) by exploring and revealing to the patient the psychogenetic processes that have resulted in conflict and maladjustment.

When I express unreserved acceptance of so much of the Freudian psychology, I may be asked from both camps: Why then do I not acknowledge myself to be a Freudian? And when I seek a concise answer to this question, I find that the main part, the principal ground, of my objection to being so classed can be expressed in

But in a recent work, *Beyond the Pleasure Principle*, he has acknowledged the primacy of the hormic principle (cp. Appendix III). I venture to assert that the rapid success of Freud's teaching, both with a large part of the medical profession and with the lay public, has been largely due to its recognition of the striving or hormic nature of man, so grossly neglected by many of our modern psychologists.

one short phrase, namely, the maintenance by the Freudians of what I shall venture to call the dogma of the Oedipus complex.

This dogma has been well called 'the ark of the Freudian covenant'. Those who accept it wholeheartedly are Freudians; those who cannot so accept it are not Freudians. It urgently behoves us, then, Freudians and non-Freudians alike, to examine as open-mindedly as possible this central feature of the Freudian doctrine which, more than anything else, is the bone of contention and the ground of the division among us.[1]

I am not going to ask our Freudian friends to give up entirely their belief in the Oedipus complex. I am going to suggest only that they may with advantage modify their doctrine in a way that will go far to resolve the deadlock, will bring about a convergence of our forces, and enable the students of human behaviour to present a united front to the scoffers and Philistines, the real enemies of the science to which we all are devoted.

OEDIPUS COMPLEX ACCEPTED IN VARIOUS FORMS BY FREUDIANS

To the casual reader of Freudian literature it may well seem that the Freudians are a compact group standing solidly together against all their many critics; and it may seem that the theory of the Oedipus complex is a clear-cut central feature of the Freudian doctrine, accepted in substantially the same form by all members of the school;

[1] Among other Freudian teachings which, in common with many others, I find unacceptable are the unrestrained and uncritical use of the principle of symbolism, the theory of dreams, the confused vague conception of the censor and the ego, and the theory of neuroses so far as it is based on the theory of the Oedipus complex.

it may seem that all alike hold the Oedipus complex, a sexual fixation on the parent of the opposite sex, to be present invariably in all human beings from early infancy, and to play a role of vast importance throughout the life of each one of us, especially in childhood and youth. But any such impression would be very wide of the truth. A closer examination of the writings of the Freudians shows that, though they all accept the theory, they accept it in widely different forms.

I propose to indicate some of these varieties, and then to examine Professor Freud's own teaching on this central topic. I mention first some psycho-analysts who may be regarded as of the straitest school.

Dr. Ernest Jones is the highest authority in Great Britain on all questions as to what is or is not orthodox psycho-analytic doctrine. In a recently published volume of lectures by six orthodox Freudians which he has edited,[1] he writes:

> We maintain that the dawn of sexual love for another person, of what is called 'object-love', is to be seen in the child's relation to its parents; in other words, that it is always at first of an incestuous nature—the so-called 'Oedipus Complex' . . . you will find that the main part of the following lectures will be taken up with tracing out the passage from these primitive incest complexes to all kinds of social activities and interests. Our theory is that the child's relation to its family remains throughout life the prototype of its relation to its fellows in general, that this exercises the profoundest influence on its character and conduct, and that the essence of the relationship is a sexual one.

And this is a literally true account of the book. The book well illustrates the enormous influence attributed

[1] *Social Aspects of Psycho-Analysis*, ed. by Dr. E. Jones, London, 1924.

to the Oedipus complex by this group of Freudians, who perhaps may be said to represent the theory in the form most widely held. One of this group, Mr. Flügel, who enjoys the distinction of being both an academic psychologist and an orthodox Freudian, has devoted a whole volume to the influence of the Oedipus complex in family relations.[1] He regards the Oedipus complex as playing an important role in all normal human life from early infancy onward.

Love for one member of the family is usually accompanied by jealousy or hatred towards some other member who possesses or is thought to possess the affections of the first. In its most typical form this conjunction of love and hate aspects occurs in the attitude of the child toward its parents. Here the dawning heterosexual inclinations of the child . . . usually bring it about that the love is directed towards the parent of the opposite sex and the hate towards the parent of the same sex as that of the child. The feelings and tendencies in question have found expression in innumerable stories, myths and legends. . . . It is more especially in the myth of Oedipus . . . that the ultimate nature of these tendencies is most openly and powerfully revealed ; and it is for this reason that the combination of the love and hate aspects with all the feelings and desires to which they give rise has come to be shortly designated as the Oedipus complex. Tendencies, which, like those revealed in the Oedipus myth and its numberless variations, have continued to manifest themselves in the productions of the popular and the artistic mind for many generations, would seem to show by their universality and tenacity that their origins lie deeply embedded in the very foundations of human life and character ; and this view of their importance is corroborated by the very significant

---

[1] Flügel, J. C. : *The Psycho-Analytic Study of the Family*, London, Psycho-Analytical Press, 1921.

place which they are found to occupy as etiological factors in the production of neuroses. Freud has gone so far as to say that the tendencies centring around the Oedipus situation form the 'nuclear complex of the neuroses', i.e., the fundamental point of conflict in the mind of the neurotic, about which the other conflicts gather and upon which they are to a great extent dependent. In the light of Freud's fruitful conception of the neuroses as due largely to the fact that a part of the emotional energy has suffered arrest at, or a regression to, a relatively early stage of mental development, this fundamental role of the Oedipus complex in the neuroses would seem to indicate that the proper development and control of the child's psychic relations to his parents constitutes at once one of the most important and one of the most difficult features of individual mental growth. That this is in fact the case has been shown both by the researches of Freud himself and by those of all other psycho-analytic investigators, and may without difficulty be confirmed by the experience of ordinary life.

The formation of the Oedipus complex is, then, in the orthodox view a normal incident of infancy; and its subsequent influence is essential, not only to the genesis of neuroses, but also to normal development; for, as Mr. Flügel goes on to say:

The early arousal of object-love in connexion with the parents ensures that these impulses shall take that direction which alone will enable the child to become a useful and a pleasant member of society.

And this all-important influence is exerted throughout life, for

Parent love not only comes into being at a very early age, but, as regards many of its attributes, it normally persists with but little alteration throughout the whole of the impressionable period from infancy to adolescence. . . . We see therefore that both as regards priority of formation and as regards duration, vigour and continuity of function throughout the all-important period of development, parent love normally occupies an almost unique place among the sentiments.

Mr. Flügel then goes on to argue that incest was probably a widespread and advantageous practice in primitive communities, and adds:

> The tendency to incest may thus be due ultimately to the action of natural selection; the long period during which incest was regularly practised may have established and ingrained it as a normal feature of the race and its persistence to-day may be due to the continuance of the hereditary disposition thus formed and thus consolidated.

For Mr. Flügel, then, the Oedipus complex, the incestuous tendency, is innate in the human race.[1]

Dr. A. A. Brill, a leading and orthodox Freudian, accepts wholeheartedly the Oedipus complex as an infantile fixation common to all neurotic and to all normal persons and as one that continues to play an important role in adult life.

> We are all destined to direct our first sexual impulses to our mothers . . . normally a repression takes place and the boy gradually projects his love to strangers. . . . In the unconscious it (the Oedipus complex) remains for ever and acts as a constant guide in the future selection of a woman.

He raises explicitly the question: 'Whether children show by their behaviour any indication of the Oedipus

[1] It is noteworthy that Freud, while he nowhere explicitly asserts that the Oedipus complex is innate, has argued in his *Totem and Taboo* and his *Group Psychology* that the sense of guilt engendered by incestuous desires of the complex is the innate foundation of all morals and religion.

complex and whether fathers realize that their sons are their rivals?' And he answers both questions affirmatively. He finds such evidence in every sign of jealousy between members of the family; making, as Freudians usually do, the implicit assumption that all jealousy is rooted in sexual attraction and rivalry. This assumption, I venture to think, is utterly unwarranted. Its only ground is that other unwarranted assumption, namely, that all love is the work of the sexual instinct.

Brill, like other Freudians, cites instances of small boys who like to sleep in the mother's bed when the father is away, and perhaps also express in words their hope that the father may be absent in order that they may be so indulged. The instances, probably equally numerous and equally capable of a non-sexual interpretation, in which a small girl likes to sleep with her mother, are consistently ignored. In a similar way one of the main difficulties of the Oedipus theory, namely, the genesis of the complex in female infants, is passed over in silence.

Dr. Kempf,[1] though not an orthodox Freudian, stands near the Freudian tradition. He attributes a vast influence to the Oedipus complex. 'The number of young men who are destroyed by incestuous love is astounding. They form a large part of the population of asylums and prisons.' He does not, I think, assert or imply either that the Oedipus complex is innate in the human species or that it is inevitably acquired by every infant. He seems, however, to believe that it is acquired by a very large proportion of all infants and that injudicious display of affection by the parent of the opposite sex may at any time during infancy or childhood bring it into being.

[1] Kempf, G. E.: *Psycho-pathology*, St. Louis, 1921.

A peculiarity of his teaching is that he makes the Oedipus complex responsible for the development of homosexuality ; whereas, as we have seen, Mr. Flügel regards it as playing a beneficent, if not an essential, role in determining the development of the inborn hetero-sexual tendency into full-blown normal heterosexuality. Dr. Kempf assumes (without showing grounds for the assumption) :

> The tendency in both males and females of the genus *homo* to regress to the homosexual level whenever the competitions and combats of heterosexual courtship or danger of hetero-sexual indulgence . . . cause fear and depression. . . . Whenever two or more men are obsessed with cravings for the affections of a certain woman, the weaker rival, who fears defeat or punishment, or cannot endure anxiety, or justify the pursuit of his craving, tends to revert back to homosexual interests if he cannot find a substitute. . . . The sexual cravings of man apparently have only comparatively recently been subjected to censorship for incestuous fixations.

It would seem that in Dr. Kempf's view homosexuality is fundamental and more primitive than heterosexuality ; that in a large proportion of children the sex impulse becomes, at various ages, directed to the parent of the opposite sex, and that in a considerable proportion of these the ensuing conflict with the parent of the same sex results in reversion to the primitive homosexuality. Dr. Kempf's views, then, are highly peculiar, and he cannot, I think, be classed with those who regard the Oedipus complex as a normal and inevitable feature of the infant's organization.

Dr. D. W. Fay has described, as ' a modern Oedipus ', a youth who undoubtedly had acquired an incestuous desire for his mother, which seems to have played a large part in bringing on a severe psychosis, though its influence was complicated by association with numerous perverts.

From the point of view of this inquiry, the notable fact about this case is that the direction of the boy's sex impulse toward his mother seems to have been brought about during adolescence by her unwise conduct. She talked freely with him about sex. When he was 13 years old, she unwittingly allowed him to see her naked; she frequently lay beside him in or on the bed.

> The elderly father became impotent at about the time the boy reached puberty. The still vigorous erotic mother turned a flood of affection on the maturing boy, overstimulating him sexually . . . after three years of both conscious and unconscious struggle against his sexual impulses, the wish for mother incest, to his horror, broke into full consciousness.[1]

But in the whole of the detailed account there is nothing that points to, or requires the assumption of, an infantile Oedipus complex. All the facts described are perfectly compatible with, and adequately explained by the assumption that the perversion was effected at puberty through the mother's unwise behaviour.

Dr. J. T. MacCurdy is a psycho-analyst who, starting from the Freudian position, has, like Dr. Kempf, refused to continue to accept all Freud's teachings. He criticizes Freud freely and does not scruple to write of the 'futile intricacies' of his reasonings. Yet he accepts the Oedipus complex whole-heartedly.

> The central theme, or plot, of this story seems to be universal; it is the Oedipus complex in one of its many adapta-

---

[1] Fay, D. W.: 'Adolf, A Modern Oedipus, *Psychoanal. Rev.* 9, 1922.

tions, often crudely expressed with literal exactness, more often modified by substituting for the parents more adult objects of interest. In the latter case, however, these surrogates are shown by the patient's speech, sooner or later, to be only substitutes.[1]

Again he writes:

It is to the genius of Freud that we owe the discovery of a theme which will rationalize much, and frequently all, of the apparently lawless productions of the mind diseased. This theme is the Oedipus complex. To the psycho-analyst it is the ark of the covenant. . . . The Oedipus complex is often defined as an unconscious wish for incestuous relations with the parent of the opposite sex, coupled with unconscious hostility toward the parent of the same sex. Conscious love and tenderness for the mother (or father) is held to be paralleled by, or based upon, an unconscious lust for sexual satisfaction in the literal sense of the term, while the antagonism for the parent of the same sex is presumed to take the form of a definitely murderous wish in the unconscious. Without an interpretation that modifies the meaning of several of these words, such a definition implies something so monstrous as to be silly. And, indeed, in actual practice, the psycho-analysts who accept such a definition with literalness belong to that class of unthinking people who cluster around any new banner and whose cries are apt to drown out the words of the real readers.[2]

Dr. MacCurdy then proceeds to redeem the hypothesis from monstrosity and silliness. He tells us that the Oedipus complex is a tendency in the unconscious in the direction of lust for the one parent and hate for the other. And this tendency is not a residue from infantile

[1] MacCurdy, J. T.: *Problems in Dynamic Psychology.*
[2] Ibid., *Psychology of Emotion*, p. 92.

experience, still less an innate part of the organization, but rather

We are forced to conclude that the Oedipus complex is not an unconscious memory but an unconscious fabrication. If an unconscious fabrication, how can it be said to exist? No mental process is directly known until it is conscious. This one is known in incomplete form in early life and in indirect expression when the subject is grown. . . . Normally, then, one might say it was known only by its effects. That which is recognized by its effects alone is a tendency. So we may safely conclude that the Oedipus complex, viewed as a definite formulation such as the word 'wish' implies, has no existence, but that viewed as a tendency the concept may have great usefulness.

From all of which it appears that for MacCurdy the Oedipus complex is, as for other psycho-analysts, 'the ark of the covenant'; but that for him it is not a complex, a definite part of the mental organization, formed in infancy and persisting through youth and adult life; but rather it is a tendency fabricated in the unconscious at or after puberty.

MacCurdy's attempt to establish a distinction between a tendency and Freud's 'unconscious wish' rooted in a complex, a fixation of the *libido*, seems to be entirely unsuccessful. However that may be, it is clear that many of the leading Freudians maintain that doctrine which MacCurdy declares to be 'so monstrous as to be silly', and that they assert it to be true not only of neurotic persons, but also of the vast majority of normal persons, and that he puts in the 'class of unthinking people who cluster round any new banner' not only Flügel, Ernest Jones, Brill and Kempf, but also Freud himself.

Dr. A. Adler and Dr. C. G. Jung are no longer to be

reckoned as members of the Freudian school. But their views on the Oedipus complex are of particular interest; for, at the time when they gave a general adhesion to Freud's theories, they presumably accepted it in Freud's sense.

Dr. Adler now contemptuously and completely rejects the theory of the Oedipus complex; writing of conflict between parents and children, he says: 'It has been magnificently misinterpreted by the Freudian school as the permanently incestuous condition of being enamoured of the mother.'

Jung, on the other hand, has transformed the theory into something entirely different. He interprets the alleged longing of the adult for a reunion with the mother as the expression of a symbolic archetype; it is to be regarded as a mystic desire for a spiritual rebirth.[1]

The teachings of psycho-analysts in regard to the Oedipus complex range all the way from the view of Flügel (according to which it is an innate constituent of the infantile mind which continues to exert a great influence, necessary to normal development, through the life of each one of us) to that of MacCurdy, according to which it is merely an adult phantasy formation, and to that of Adler, according to which it is merely a 'magnificent misinterpretation'.

I turn now to Professor Freud's own writings, the fountain head from which have sprung the diverse streams

[1] It is difficult to define Jung's position on this question; but his increasingly accentuated repudiation of infantile sexuality makes it clear that he cannot be said to accept the Oedipus complex in the usual Freudian form. In one passage he writes: 'The incest complex is much more a purely regressive production of phantasies than a reality' (*The Theory of Psycho-analysis*).

which we have tried to follow in the writings of some of his principal disciples. We find there the sources of all these streams, and more besides.

OEDIPUS COMPLEX ESTABLISHED IN INFANCY

In the *Three Contributions to the Sexual Theory*, we are taught that the sexual impulse or instinct 'is probably entirely independent of its object and does not depend on the stimuli of the same for its origin'. That is to say, the impulse is inborn; but, as laid down in the constitution, it is not directed to any object and is capable of becoming directed to any one of many different objects. The direction to an object, 'the object finding', is in the main determined by the stimulation of erogenous zones; those objects which stimulate any one of many erogenous zones become objects of the sexual impulse. Of such objects the mother's body is normally one of principal importance. For the lips are an erogenous zone, and the libidinous pleasure which the infant obtains in suckling at the breast directs the impulse to this object.

> While the very incipient sexual gratifications are still connected with the taking of nourishment, the sexual impulse has a sexual object outside its own body in his mother's breast. . . . It is not without good reason that the suckling of the child from its mother's breast has become a model for every amour. The object-finding is really a refinding.

Again:

> The intercourse between the child and its foster-parents is for the former an inexhaustible source of sexual excitation and gratification of erogenous zones, especially since the parents—or as a rule the mother—supplies the child with feelings which originate from her own sexual life; she pats it, kisses it, and rocks it, plainly taking it as a substitute for

a full-valued sexual object. . . . All her tenderness awakens the sexual impulse of her child and prepares its future intensity.

Thus is formed the Oedipus complex of the boy infant. How that of the girl infant is formed, how her infantile sex impulse becomes directed on the father, in spite of her erogenous contact with her mother—on this problem Freud throws no light, beyond hinting that the father (presumably in consequence of his infantile lust for his mother) prefers his daughters to his sons and lavishes on them more tenderness and caresses.

In this work (dating from before 1910, the year of the English translation) Freud implies that the Oedipus complex, once formed in early infancy, not only becomes the nucleus of the unconscious and the source of all or most of the psychoneuroses, but also exerts important influences in the later life of all normal persons.[1]

In the phantasies of all persons the infantile inclinations, now re-enforced by the somatic emphasis, reappear, and among them one finds in lawful frequency and in the first place the sexual feeling of the child for the parents. This has usually already been differentiated by the sexual attraction, the attraction of the son for the mother and of the daughter for the father. . . . This shows that the apparently non-sexual love for the parents and the sexual love are nourished

---

[1] Jung correctly describes Freud's earlier teaching on this topic by saying: 'He takes the tendency towards incest to be an absolute concrete sexual wish, lacking only the quality of consciousness. He calls this complex the root complex, or nucleus, of the neuroses, and is inclined, viewing this as the original one, to reduce nearly the whole psychology of the neuroses, as well as many other phenomena in the world of mind, to this complex.' (*The Theory of Psycho-analysis.*)

from the same source, i.e., that the first merely corresponds to an infantile fixation of *libido*. . . . When a once healthy person merges into disease after an unhappy love-affair, the mechanism of the disease can distinctly be explained as a return of his *libido* to the persons preferred in his infancy.

In this work we are led to believe that the infantile fixation of the *libido* on the parent of the opposite sex is repressed into the unconscious by the prohibition, the incest barriers, erected by society.

It would of course be most natural for the child (at puberty) to select as the sexual object that person whom it has loved since childhood with, so to speak, a suppressed *libido*. But, owing to the delay of sexual maturity, time has been gained for the erection beside the sexual inhibitions of the incest barrier, the moral prescription which explicitly excludes from the object selection the beloved persons of infancy or blood relation. The observance of this barrier is above all a demand of cultural society which must guard against the absorption by the family of those interests which it needs for the production of higher social units.

This language leaves open, with a most tantalizing ambiguity, the questions: Is the incest barrier innate? —Or is it a product in the individual of social prohibitions? But, since Freud here tells us that the sex impulse is not innately directed to the opposite sex, it is fair to assume that the incest barrier is not meant to be innate. For it would seem in the last degree improbable that in a species in which the sexual impulse is not innately directed to the opposite sex, there should have been evolved an innate barrier against sexual direction of the boy toward the mother, or of the girl toward the father.

In this respect Mr. Flügel appears to have departed from the teaching of Freud, in assuming both an innate direction of the sex-instinct toward the opposite sex, and an innate incest barrier. If so, he was but anticipating his master; for in his later writings, Freud has inclined more and more to the postulation of racial complexities of constitution as explanatory principles, especially in respect of the incest barrier. In fact, much of his later speculation makes of an assumed innate incest barrier a principle foundation stone of far-reaching sociologic theories.

I find some advance in this direction in 'Introductory Lectures on Psycho-analysis', lectures delivered in 1915–17. Here the Oedipus complex plays an important role at puberty and in adult life.

The deepest and most common motive for estrangement, especially between parent and child of the same sex, came into play in the earliest years of childhood. I refer to that rivalry of affections in which sexual elements are plainly emphasized. The son, when quite a little child, already begins to develop a peculiar tenderness toward his mother, whom he looks upon as his own property, regarding his father in the light of a rival who disputes this sole possession of his; similarly the little daughter sees in her mother some one who disturbs her tender relation to her father and occupies a place which she feels she herself could very well fill. Observation shows us how far back these sentiments date, sentiments which we describe by the term Oedipus complex. . . . I do not assert that the Oedipus complex exhausts all the possible relations which may exist between parents and children; these relations may well be a great deal more complicated. Again, this complex may be more or less strongly developed, or it may even become inverted, but it is a regular and very important factor in the mental life of the child; we are more in danger of underestimating than of overestimating its influence and that of the developments which may follow from it. . . . So we look for the Oedipus complex even in those dreamers who have been fortunate enough to escape conflicts with their parents in later life.

Then comes a hint of the innate incest barrier.

Psycho-analytic investigations have shown beyond the possibility of doubt that *an incestuous love-choice* is in fact the first and the regular one, that it is only later that any opposition is manifested towards it, the causes of which are not to be sought in the psychology of the individual (p. 175).

This is a cryptic and baffling sentence ; but in view of the fact that *Totem and Taboo* was published before the date of these lectures, I think we may interpret it as a hint of the innateness of the incest barrier. For in *Totem and Taboo* we are offered an account of the psychogenesis of the sense of guilt, an innate reaction of the male of the species to his incestuous desire for his mother, the disposition to this reaction being impressed on the species by the severities of a long succession of brutal and tyrannical horde-fathers. 'The sense of guilt of mankind as a whole, which is the ultimate source of religion and morality, was acquired in the beginning of history through the Oedipus complex.' In the *Lectures* Freud is quite explicit as to the universal continued and far-reaching influence in later life of the Oedipus complex.

Sucking at the mother's breast becomes the point of departure from which the whole sexual life develops, the unattainable prototype of every later sexual satisfaction, to which in times of need phantasy often enough reverts. The desire to suck includes within it the desire for the mother's breast, which is therefore the first *object* of sexual desire ; I cannot convey to you any adequate idea of the importance of this first object in determining every later object adopted, of the profound influence it exerts, through transformation and substitution, upon the most distant fields of mental life.

For the desire for the mother's breast develops in early childhood into a distinctly sexual desire for the mother. At about 3 years of age, we are told, the diffuse sexuality of the infant becomes more explicitly genital ; and ' before the latency period (which begins about the sixth year) the object adopted proves almost identical with the first object of the oral pleasure impulse—it is, namely, the mother, although not the mother's breast '.

FREUD CHANGES HIS VIEWS CONCERNING OEDIPUS COMPLEX

Freud then deals with the suggestion that perhaps, after all, the alleged evidence of the Oedipus complex yielded by neurotic patients is a phantasy formation only (as asserted by Jung and MacCurdy) and decisively rejects it.

We soon discover, too, that the hatred against the father has been strengthened by a number of motives arising in later periods and other relationships in life, and that the sexual desires towards the mother had been moulded into forms which would have been as yet foreign to the child. But it would be a vain attempt if we endeavoured to explain the whole of the Oedipus complex by ' retrogressive phantasy-making ', and by motives originating in later periods of life. The infantile nucleus, with more or less of the accretions to it, remains intact.

And at puberty :

When the sexual instinct first asserts its demands in full strength, the old familiar incestuous objects are taken up again and again invested by the *libido*. The infantile object-choice was but a feeble venture in play, as it were, but it laid down the direction for the object-choice of puberty. At this time a very intense flow of feeling toward the Oedipus complex or in reaction from it comes into force ; since their mental antecedents have become intolerable, however, these feelings must remain for the most part outside consciousness. From the time of puberty onward the human individual must devote himself to the great task of freeing himself from the parents ; and only after this detachment is accomplished can he cease to be a child and so become a member of the social community. For a son, the task consists in releasing his libidinal desires from his mother . . . and in reconciling himself with his father . . . these tasks are laid down for every man.

And in the lectures the tendency to postulate numerous and specific innate dispositions, first clearly manifested in *Totem and Taboo,* is carried much further. For in this work, not only the sense of guilt, but also a large range of primal phantasies are regarded as innate in the species. As these primal phantasies are largely concerned with the sex activities of infancy, it would seem an inevitable corollary that, far from regarding the sex impulses as undirected in the infant prior to experience, Freud must now regard the Oedipus complex itself as innate.

In a paper of 1920, ' Homosexuality in a Woman ', Freud makes free use of the Oedipus complex, and derives the patient's homosexuality by the following devious process. The patient is supposed to have suffered the usual infantile fixation on the father. At puberty this becomes increasingly active and generates a strong desire for a child by her father.

She became keenly conscious of the wish to have a child, and a male one ; that it was her father's child and his image that she desired, her consciousness was not allowed to know. And then it was not she who bore the child, but the unconsciously hated rival, her mother. Furiously resentful and embittered, she turned away from her father, and from men altogether. . . . She changed into a man and took her mother in place of her father as her love-object.

But her mother was hostile and inaccessible to her; therefore she chose another woman older than herself and became passionately attached to her; and this in defiance of her father's displeasure, for in this way she took her revenge on her father for her disappointment. 'Henceforth she remained homosexual out of defiance against her father.'

This surely is a most devious course of the *libido*. The account taxes our credulity most severely: especially in view of the fact that the woman to whom she became attached is described as displaying distinctly masculine traits. It is then with astonishment that the reader, or at least one reader, finds, toward the end of the long account of this case, the following passage: 'deeper consideration of the material undertaken later impels us to conclude that it is rather a case of inborn homosexuality which, as usual, became fixed and unmistakably manifest only in the period following puberty'.

The central importance of the Oedipus complex in Freud's view is further illustrated by his theory of 'the transference', which plays an all-important part in his therapy. For in 'the transference' the physician becomes, according to this theory, a temporary substitute for the parent; the *libido* fixated on the parent, in the form of the Oedipus complex, is transferred to the physician; thus and then only is the Oedipus complex deprived of its power over the patient.

A FURTHER GREAT CHANGE OF FREUD'S VIEW

I turn now to a recent article by Freud which reveals further and great changes in his view of the Oedipus complex. I am not one of those who reproach an author when they find evidence that his views have changed. It is to my thinking one of Professor Freud's great merits, that he has the courage to develop, and even to make radical changes in, his teaching. The change which I now wish to point out consists in nothing less than the admission that *the Oedipus complex has no existence in normal adolescent and adult persons.* Freud nowhere asserts this explicitly; but its absence from normal persons is clearly implied in the following passages:

The significance of the Oedipus complex as the central phenomenon of the sexual period in early childhood reveals itself more and more. After this it disappears: it *succumbs to repression*, as we say, and is followed by the latency period. But it is not yet clear to us what occasions *its decay*; analyses seem to show that the painful disappointments experienced bring this about. The little girl who wants to believe herself her father's partner in love must one day endure a harsh punishment at his hands, and find herself hurled to earth from her cloud-castles. The boy who regards his mother as his own property finds that her love and care for him are transferred to a new arrival. Reflection deepens the effect of these impressions by insisting that painful experiences of this kind, antagonistic to the content of the complex, are inevitable. Even when no special events such as those mentioned occur, the absence of the hoped-for gratification, the continual frustration of the wish of the child, causes the lovelorn little one to turn from its hopeless longing. According to this, the Oedipus complex *becomes extinguished* by its lack of success, the result of its inherent impossibility. Another view would put it that the Oedipus complex *must come to an end* because the time has come for its *dissolution*, just as the milk-teeth fall out when the permanent ones begin to press forward. Although *the majority of human children individually pass through the Oedipus complex*, yet after all it is a phenomenon determined and laid down for them by heredity and must decline according to schedule when the next preordained stage of development arrives. It is therefore not very important what the occasions are through which this happens or whether any such occasions are discoverable at all.

One cannot dispute the justice of both these views. They are compatible with each other; moreover, there is room for the ontogenetic alongside the more far-reaching phylogenetic one.[1]

Freud thus accepts both views, the view that the genesis and decay of the Oedipus complex are alike processes of maturation, predetermined in the hereditary constitution, and the view that these innately determined processes are facilitated and promoted by individual experiences. In his earlier writings[2] Freud regarded the innate sexual impulse as entirely devoid of direction to any kind of object and attributed the formation of the boy's Oedipus complex to the sexual satisfaction which he obtained through suckling at his mother's breast, and through the sexual stimulation which the mother's ministrations to his bodily needs are alleged unavoidably to bring. Now, in accordance with his more recent tendency to seek explanations in hereditary constitution, Freud seems inclined to regard the Oedipus complex as innate, as appearing in the infant by an inevitable process of maturation. This avoids a difficulty which I pointed out many years ago, namely, the genesis of the Oedipus complex in the girl, who normally goes through, in relation to her father, no such erogenous contacts as the boy infant is supposed to suffer in his relations with his mother. Nevertheless, Freud is not content with the

[1] Freud, S.: 'The Passing of the Oedipus Complex', *Internat. J. Psycho-Anal.* 5, 1924.—Italics are mine.

[2] Especially *Three Contributions to Sexual Theory.*

maturation theory of the decay of the Oedipus complex and sets out to explain it ontogenetically, i.e., to discover the individual experiences which normally bring about this decay. The conclusion he reaches is ' that the boy's Oedipus complex succumbs to the dread of castration '. Since the reasoning by which Freud reaches this conclusion illuminates vividly his more recent teaching on infantile sexuality it is worth while to present it here.

When the (male) child's interest turns to his genital organ, he betrays this by handling it frequently, and then he is bound to discover that grown-up people do not approve of this activity. More or less plainly and more or less brutally, the threat is uttered that this high-valued part of him will be taken away.

Here it is necessary to remind the reader that these are assumed to be typical experiences necessary to the normal development of the boy infant.

Now the view we hold is that the phallic stage of the genital organization succumbs to this threat of castration. But not immediately, and not without the assistance of further influences; for, to begin with, the boy does not believe in the threat nor obey it in the least. . . . The observation that finally breaks down the child's unbelief is the sight of the female genitalia. Some day or other it happens that the child, whose own penis is such a proud possession, obtains a sight of the genital parts of a little girl; he must then become convinced of the absence of a penis in a creature so like himself. With this, however, the loss of his own penis becomes imaginable, and the threat of castration achieves its delayed effect . . . we cannot overlook the fact that the child's sexual life at this time is by no means exhausted by masturbation. The child is demonstrably under the influence of the Oedipus attitude to its parents; masturbation is only the discharge in the genitals of the excitation belonging to the complex, and to this connexion between the two masturbation will owe its significance ever after. The Oedipus complex offered the child two possibilities of satisfaction, an active and a passive one. It could put itself in its father's place and have intercourse with the mother as he did, so that the father was soon felt to be an obstacle; or else it wanted to supplant the mother and be loved by the father, whereon the mother became superfluous. The child may have had only the vaguest notion of what constituted the love-intercourse which serves as a gratification, but that the penis played a part in it was certain, for the feelings in his own organ were evidence of that. So far there had been no occasion for doubt about a penis in women. But now the acceptance of the possibility of castration, the recognition that women are castrated, makes an end of both the possibilities of satisfaction in the Oedipus complex. For both of them—the male as a consequence, a punishment, and the other, the female, as a pre-requisite —would indeed be accompanied by the loss of the penis.

We are left in doubt whether these painful reflections on the part of the male infant are supposed to take place consciously or in the unconscious, presumably the latter. But, in either case, the course of events alleged to be usual and necessary for the normal development of every male infant would seem to be as follows: The infant through masturbation and the pleasant feelings accompanying the process learns to value his penis very highly. About the same time his *libido* becomes fixated on his mother by reason of the sexual gratifications he obtains through contacts with her person; or alternately or subsequently, for reasons not given, the male infant may learn to desire sexual gratification from the father (perhaps this is due to the maturation of an innate homosexuality, the alleged homosexual component of the sex instinct). Then come threats of castration; which becomes effective only when the boy learns that the female has no penis. In cases of the former type, the threat of castration becomes effective, because it is a threat to deprive the boy of his much-valued penis. In the other type of infant, no such threat is needed; he desires to get rid of his penis in order to serve as female partner to his father; a conflict between this desire and his desire to retain his valued penis results. In the infant confronting this painful dilemma, the desire to retain the penis gains the upper hand over the opposing desire; therefore the Oedipus complex, in which the latter desire is rooted, decays and *succumbs*; 'the child's ego turns away from the Oedipus complex'.

FREUD ADMITS ABSENCE OF OEDIPUS COMPLEX IN NORMAL ADULTS

Freud continues:

I have described elsewhere the way by which this aversion is accomplished. The object-cathexes are given up and replaced by identification. The authority of the father or the parents is introjected into the ego, and there forms the kernel of the super-ego, which takes its severity from the father, perpetuates his prohibition against incest, and so ensures the ego against a recurrence of the libidinal object-cathexis. The libidinal trends belonging to the Oedipus complex are in part desexualized or sublimated, which probably happens with every transformation into identification; in part they are inhibited in their aim and changed into affectionate feelings. The whole process, on the one hand, preserves the genital organ, wards off the danger of losing it; on the other hand, it paralyses it, takes away its function from it. This process introduces the latency period, which now interrupts the child's sexual development. I see no reason to deny the name of 'repression' to the ego's turning from the Oedipus complex, although later repressions are for the most part effected with the participation of the super-ego, which is only built up during this process. But the process described is more than a repression; when carried out in the ideal way, it is equivalent to a *destruction and abrogation* of the complex. It is not a great step to assume that here we have come upon the borderland between normal and pathological which is never very sharply defined. If the ego has really not achieved much more than a repression of the complex, then this latter persists unconsciously in the *id* and will express itself later on in some pathogenic effect.

The last sentence seems to me especially instructive. It amounts to the admission of a view which I have long held, namely, that in the normal healthy person there is no Oedipus complex; whereas in a certain number of persons, such a complex is a reality, and that these persons are those who for obvious reasons are highly susceptible to neurotic troubles. Further, this view, now adopted by Freud, harmonizes perfectly with a suggestion which I made many years ago, namely, that there are very great individual differences in respect to the age at which the sex-instinct becomes in any degree operative; that in normally constituted persons it begins to play some part in mental life at about the eighth year, whereas in a minority, it becomes active earlier, perhaps even in the first years, as Freud asserts for all infants.[1] The latter group would then be those liable to the formation of the Oedipus complex and peculiarly likely to develop neuroses later in life and therefore to come into the hands of the psycho-analysts.

But, as regards the former group, those who, as Freud says, develop ' in the ideal way ' and who as adults have no Oedipus complex, why should we not be content with

[1] Jung sustains this view by referring to cases of female infants with normal menstruation at 2 years of age and of boys of 3 and 4 years having normal erections.

the obvious interpretation that they never had an Oedipus complex? What justifies Freud's assumption that all human beings, healthy and neurotic alike, develop the Oedipus complex in infancy, and that the healthy get rid of it completely while the neurotic, failing to get rid of it, retains it, repressed but active in the unconscious?

Since this relatively simple view that only a certain limited number of persons acquire an Oedipus complex, in many of whom it becomes a source of conflict and disorder, since this view comports with all the facts, what justification remains for the Freudian assumption that in all infants, those destined to remain healthy, as well as those destined to become neurotic, the Oedipus complex develops 'as the central phenomenon' of early childhood?

So far as I can follow the Freudian reasoning, the evidence of the reality of the Oedipus complex consists in the conflicts in which it plays its part in the adult. And, according to his earlier teaching, evidence of the Oedipus complex in healthy persons is found in their dreams. But Freud himself now tells us that those adults who have followed an ideal way of development, that is to say normal adults, have no Oedipus complex; in them he tells us it has '*succumbed* or has been *extinguished* by its lack of success', has *come to an end*, has undergone *abrogation* and *dissolution*. Why then assert that it was present in them during infancy, and proceed to construct a most fanciful theory to account for its decay and extinction? For the evidence of its presence in infancy formerly alleged was its influence on the dreams of the adult. How much more satisfactory to admit that, as there is no evidence of its existence in these normal adults, there is no ground to infer its existence in their infancy?

FREUD RETAINS BELIEF IN OEDIPUS COMPLEX OF CHILDREN

Since Freud now admits that there is no Oedipus complex in the normal adult, the grounds of the assertion of the existence of the Oedipus complex in infants who later become normal adults seem to be simply the following: (1) the general implicit assumption that as many phenomena of human life as possible must be referred to the sex instinct; (2) the fact that children not infrequently display some affection for their parents; for, according to Freud, all love, in the sense other than the directly sexual inclination, all tender feeling, all tender affection, is derived from the sexual instinct, by way of a conversion of a part of the *libido*, a conversion which occurs when its more directly sexual expressions are repressed. But this strange theory of the origin of tender feeling or emotion is in its turn derived from the theory of the universal presence of the Oedipus complex in infancy. And so the reasoning is completely circular and of no value.

Any such frank avowal that the assumption of the Oedipus complex in all infants was erroneous and ill-based would greatly simplify Freud's psychology of the male infant and relieve him of the necessity of making the fantastic assumption that the normal development of all boys depends on the castration threat or on their acquiring a homosexual desire for the father; these being, according to his account, the two alternative conditions of the extinction of the Oedipus complex. It would also relieve him of great difficulties in respect of the female infant. Freud would seem recently to have become aware of these difficulties, some of which I pointed out in the paper referred to above.[1] He remarks: 'We must attend to a question which . . . has long been left on one side. The process described [that of extinction of the Oedipus complex in normal boys] relates, as we expressly stated, only to the male child. How is the corresponding development effected in the little girl? Freud at least has the merit of frankly avowing the difficulty in regard to the decay of the Oedipus complex in the female; though he still ignores the more real difficulty of accounting for its genesis in the female infant. 'Here', he writes, 'our material—for some reason we do not understand—becomes far more shadowy and incomplete.' He asserts, nevertheless, that 'the female sex develops an Oedipus complex too, a super-ego and a latency period'. Are we to take this assertion as being made of the female sex in general, or of some members of it, perhaps of those only who are destined to be neurotic? It is impossible to say. This is one of those many instances of ambiguity of language which makes it so difficult to bring effective criticism to bear. However, it would seem that the statement is meant to be of general application to the female sex; for Freud thereupon sets out in search of a theory of the destruction of the Oedipus complex in the female child. Clearly 'the castration dread' cannot serve here; for the girl believes herself to be already castrated, 'she accepts castration as an established fact, an operation already performed'. The process of destruction of the Oedipus complex seems 'to be due in the girl far more than in the boy to the results of educative influences, of external intimidation threatening the loss of love. The Oedipus

[1] 'The Definition of the Sexual Instinct', *Proc. Royal Soc. Med.* 7, 1914.

complex in the girl is far simpler, less equivocal, than that of the little possessor of the penis ; in my experience it seldom goes beyond the wish to take the mother's place, the feminine attitude towards the father.' But,

> Acceptance of the loss of the penis is not endured without some attempt at compensation. The girl passes over—by way of a symbolic analogy one may say—from the penis to a child ; her Oedipus complex culminates in the desire, which is long cherished, to be given a child by her father as a present, to bear him a child. One has the impression that the Oedipus complex is later gradually abandoned because this wish is never fulfilled. . . . The comparative weakness of the sadistic component of the sexual instinct which may probably be related to the penis-deficiency, facilitates the transformation of directly sexual trends into those inhibited in aim, feelings of tenderness.

Here once more Freud resolutely refuses to contemplate the possibility that the ' feelings of tenderness ' of the girl may be due to the working within her of a maternal instinct, an instinct manifested so clearly by so many animals (I think one may safely say by all female mammals and nearly all female birds) in complete independence of, and in entirely different manner from, the working of the sex-instinct.

Freud concludes that ' it must be confessed, however, that on the whole our insight into these processes of development in the girl is unsatisfying, shadowy and incomplete '. With this verdict every unbiased reader will surely agree, and not a few of us would extend it to the Freudian account of the alleged working of the castration dread in the boy.

I submit that this discussion of the Oedipus complex by Freud amounts to virtual admission by him that the assumption of the presence of the Oedipus complex in all children was mistaken. I urge that the error should be frankly avowed. It is true that to take that step would be very difficult, would require much courage. For it has become a leading dogma of his school that the Oedipus complex is the very kernel and most active and important constituent of the unconscious in all mankind. Freud himself has given countenance to this assumption and has used it widely; as, for example, in his *Totem and Taboo* and in his *Group Psychology*, in which books it is made to appear as the root of all religion and morality, as the generator of that sense of guilt which is assumed by him to play a fundamental role in these developments. So clearly has Freud implied this in his earlier writings, and he and his followers have built so much on this assumption, that I, for one, experienced something of a shock when I found in the article under discussion that Freud no longer holds this assumption, but describes the Oedipus complex as succumbing, as undergoing decay and extinction, in the course of normal development. But my shock must be mild compared to that which many of Freud's followers must have suffered. For they must surely for some brief moments suspect that this article of their master's, if it does not actually and truly describe, 'the passing of the Oedipus complex', does at least foreshadow that considerable and even momentous event in the future course of psycho-analytic theory.

COMMENT

I urge, then, that psycho-analysts should follow their leader in this radical change of view—that they should frankly repudiate the doctrine that the Oedipus complex exists in normal adults; and that they should at the same time go further and, recognizing that the evidence for the universality of the Oedipus complex in infancy was its alleged influence in adolescence and in adult life, should be content to assume that it occurs only in those infants who later develop neurotic symptoms that clearly point to it.

I am prepared to believe that an Oedipus complex may be formed very early in life in some unfortunate persons. For, as I argued in my paper of 1914, there is reason to believe that the sex instinct first begins to influence the mental life at very different ages in different persons. A large amount of evidence points to the seventh or eighth year as the time at which it first begins to stir in the majority of children. But it is probable that its maturation may attain this point much earlier in some children, perhaps even in the first year, and that these individuals are destined to, or most liable to, develop neurotic disorders in later life.

I would in this connexion point out that the manifestation of unmistakable sexual attraction toward the parent of opposite sex on the part of an adult or adolescent is in itself no evidence of the formation of an Oedipus complex in infancy. Such instances undoubtedly occur and perhaps are not rare. But in such instances it will, I think, usually be found that influences exerted during adolescence sufficiently and completely account for the condition. This certainly is true of Dr. Fay's case of *Adolf, a Modern Oedipus.* And it is noteworthy that the same is true of the single case of the kind described by Freud in his *Lectures.*[1] The patient, a girl of 19, did show an erotic attachment to her father, which seems to have been the root of her trouble. This patient had

[1] Freud, S.: Seventeenth Lecture. Similar instances are also described by Brill. In one case the boy was accustomed to sleep in the same bed with his mother up to 10 years of age, in another up to 18 years.

been allowed to sleep in bed between her father and her mother and to continue this practice until ' she finally grew too big to be comfortable in the same bed with the parents ' ; and even after this time ' she achieved the same thing by consciously simulating fear and getting her mother to change places with her and to give up to her her place by her father. This incident was undoubtedly the starting-point of phantasies.' If parents behave toward adolescents in the reckless fashion of Adolf's mother and of the parents of this girl, such sexual attractions can hardly fail to be generated ; but they are quite intelligible without the postulation of an infantile Oedipus complex ; and every such instance weakens, rather than strengthens, the case for the Oedipus complex as an infantile formation.

We have found, then, that the psycho-analysts of the Freudian school entertain the most diverse views about this ' ark of the covenant ', the Oedipus complex ; ranging from the view that it is innately present in every infant of the human species to the view that it is a phantasy formation of later life, and the latest view of Freud himself that it has no existence in the normal adolescent and adult. If they will frankly take the next step, so plainly indicated, and admit that it (the infantile Oedipus complex) is a peculiarity of some of those infants who later become neurotic, they will go far toward making possible that reconciliation between psycho-analytic theory and academic psychology which is so much to be desired, and toward which I hope this paper may contribute in some slight degree.

APPENDIX V

SOME SOCIAL EFFECTS OF THE FREUDIAN TEACHINGS

I AM loth to seem to find arguments for the rejection of Freudian errors by pointing to their evil social consequences. In the text I have been content to rest the case purely on considerations of truth and evidence. In this brief appendix I seek merely to emphasize the importance of correcting these errors, if errors they be. And my argument runs as follows: the Freudian teaching has had and is still exercising most destructive effects throughout our Western civilization, destructive both of the happiness of a multitude of individuals and of the moral traditions of society; and these deplorable effects flow, not at all from the truths which Freud has revealed, but from the errors which he has expounded with such fateful success, as well as from popular misinterpretations, of his strangely intimate blend of truth and error.

To substantiate these statements with any convincing evidence is hardly possible. In such matters there is wide scope for differences of opinion. But I must try to make my charge more specific.

I do not regard Freud's somewhat childish attack on religion as of much importance in this respect. Perhaps the materialistic and strictly deterministic character generally claimed for his psychology is of some considerable influence, in the way of giving a kind of pseudo-respectability to popular materialism, fatalism, and hedonism, and thus abetting all their paralysing and deteriorating tendencies. Yet this also is of secondary importance: for Freud's psychology is intrinsically neither materialistic, nor deterministic, nor hedonist. In so far as these qualities are read into it, it is because the prejudices of the author peep through his teaching.

More seriously destructive of happiness and sound traditions has been the pan-sexual doctrine—especially the doctrine of the Oedipus complex.

This has worked in two ways to spoil the relations between parents and children, relations which are so essential to the flourishing of the family and of all our culture and civilization. On the one hand, parents have been made fearful of manifesting the least affection for their children (having been taught that all such manifestations are libidinous, are sexual displays which must inevitably provoke sexual responses from the children and promote the formation of the dread Oedipus complex). This is true of Europe, but even more extensively true of America, where every fad is ridden to an extreme. In this connexion Dr. Sheldon (op. cit.) writes:

> In the past half-dozen years I have again and again had to assure parents who have been through college, that it is 'all right' to show a little spontaneity and playfulness and delight, even a little affection, in their relations with their young children. These people, in their silly and credulous horror of the Oedipus complex, had proceeded to shut and bolt all the doors and windows that lead to maturation in the higher panels of consciousness. They are comparable to children I have known who, their heads filled with tales of the bogyman, missed all of the mystery and the beauty of the night.

On the other hand, the young people have been taught that their chief moral duty, an essential condition of their attainment of maturity, is strict avoidance of all manifestation of respect, affection, sympathy or esteem for their parents. Even the relatively wise Jung prints in this connexion quite a lot of foolishness about the biological duties of the young person and how they can only be achieved by the repudiation of the natural ties between parent and child.

For my part, even if I were convinced of the truth of the pan-sexual doctrine, I should still rate highly the moral worth and beauty of filial devotion ; yes, even in those cases in which it results in neglect of the 'biological duty' of copulation and reproduction.

The relations between the generations are already endangered by the many violent changes of the social order which we owe to physical science. It is for psychology to prevent, to provide against and to rectify the disastrous consequences of these too violent and disruptive social changes. But instead, the Freudian psychology has worked as an additional disruptive force, especially among the strata of our communities which more than any others have the power and the function of moulding social tradition and practice.

In yet another way the Freudian teaching has been socially destructive, namely, it has greatly favoured a phenomenon which Dr. Sheldon happily describes as the emergence of the waster mind to dominance in our civilization. He writes :

> The real enemies of character are not to be found among atheists or critics of religion or non-conformists, but they are lusty noise-loving expressionists, who believe in living for the moment, in having their fling, and who say, 'Let's have no more long faces, no inhibitions and no wet blankets at our party.'
>
> They are the good livers, unchastened, unreverent souls.

Popularly they have become associated with the term extravert, though it would be more meaningful to call them the feebly inhibited. They live at the surface of awareness and are dissociated from their own deeper consciousness. They have moved sharply away from the principle of reminiscent contemplation, and have gravitated far over toward the principle of extreme sensuality, thus dissociating the conscious focus from the deeper levels. They perforce seek overstimulation, love city life, and have a profound terror of the inferiority complex. Their God is Expression, and their spiritual counsellors are the Freudian psycho-analysts. Flushed with the successful overthrow of Christian theology, they are resolved to smash away all that was ever associated with the spiritual, or religious, or reminiscent, or chastened mental outlook; their exultant ecstasy—their mystic experience—consequently finds its only channels of expression in the processes of getting things, of social domination, and of sexual diffusion.

This contemporary phenomenon, the predominance of the waster mind, is a far more serious matter than the present economic chaos; for it is far more fundamental. It is a main cause or condition of that chaos. The American economic boom and slump of 1929 was one of its most striking and unmistakable manifestations.

And there can be no doubt that the errors of the Freudian psychology (together with various popular misinterpretations of it, especially the popular identification of all self-control and restraint with repression) have vastly promoted this emergence of the waster mind to dominance; and that in two ways chiefly. First, the overemphasis on sex, and on the importance of sex expression and of sex relations of all kinds. Practically, Freud's teaching, filtered and distorted in many ways, works upon the multitude as a precept against all restraint in sex matters. He seems to the man in the street to say—You are all sex, whatever you do is sexually motivated; and frank expressions of sex are very much preferable in every way to disguised expressions. Therefore be frankly sexual, and you will be both happy and healthy. Restrain your sex impulse at your peril; that way lies neurotic disorder and insanity.

This more direct incitement to 'self-expression', to the living out of one's natural tendencies, is re-enforced by a second deduction (however doubtfully legitimate) from the Freudian psychology, namely, that all restraint, inhibition, self-control involves repression, and all repression is bad; therefore never restrain your impulses, never check your children, and be sure to send them to a school where they will be allowed to do exactly as and when they please. This is the way the waster mind is cultivated, especially in America, so effectively and on so large a scale as to result in its present dominance of the social and economic scene.

INDEX

Printed in Great Britain by
Butler & Tanner Ltd.,
Frome and London